Cooking from My Heart

LOVING SPOONFULS FROM
A SRI LANKAN FAMILY KITCHEN

*To Doreen
with lots of love.
Hope you'll enjoy these Recipes
Swarna.*

Swarna Sugunasiri

*December 13, 2008
Toronto.*

AuthorHouse™
1663 Liberty Drive, Suite 200
Bloomington, IN 47403
www.authorhouse.com
Phone: 1-800-839-8640

©2008 Swarna Sugunasiri. All rights reserved.

No part of this book may be reproduced, stored in a retrieval system, or transmitted by any means without the written permission of the author.

First published by AuthorHouse   11/24/2008

ISBN: 978-1-4389-1746-7 (sc)

Printed in the United States of America
Bloomington, Indiana

This book is printed on acid-free paper.

authorHOUSE®

Dedication

This book is dedicated to
my mom, Marynona,
and dad, James,
for implanting a love of food in me.

Swarna boiling milk at her house-warming over a temporary 3-brick hearth set-up in her living room in Sri Lanka

CONTENTS

Preface ix

SAVORIES

Beef Patties 2
For Pastry 3
Fish Cutlets 4
Lentil Fritters 6

BRUNCH

ONE   Opener 10
TWO   Fruit, Nut N' Yogurt Melange 10
THREE   Savories 11
FOUR   Basic Batter For Hoppers 12
FIVE   A Final Touch! 12

FRESH SALADS

Low-fat But Creamy Dressing 16
Apple-turnip Salad 17
Asparagus, Green Beans, Carrot & Beet Salad 18
Coleslaw With Anise & Dry Mustard Powder 19
Cucumber & Yogurt Salad 20
Deep-fried Anchovy (Dried Sprats) Salad 21
Deep-fried Bittergourd Salad 22
Iceberg Lettuce Salad #1 24
Iceberg Lettuce Salad #2 25
Orange Perfumed Warm Couscous Salad 26
Parsley Salad 28
Romaine Lettuce Salad With Honey Garlic Dressing 29
Salad For Two - With Pears, Anise, Tomato & Onions (Red N' White) ... 30
Tomato & Purple Onion Salad 31

MALLUNG: DRY-COOKED SALADS

Cabbage Mallung, Using Savoy Cabbage 34
Collard Mallung 36
Kale Mallung 38
Polos-gaeta (Young Jack-fruit) Mallung 40

VEGETABLE CURRIES

Ash Plantain* Curry 44
Black Eye Peas With Mixed Vegetables 46
Cadju [Cashew] Curry 47
Caramalized Fennel & Onion , In Tamarind Sauce. 48
Cucumber White Curry 50
Curried Blackbeans With Leftover Roasted Vegetables! 52
Mixed Capsicum Chillies Curried 53
Curried Eggplant, With Chickpeas & Sweet Bell Pepper 54
Curried Eggplant, With Peppers & Onions 56
Currried Eggplants, Cubernale Peppers and Onions. 58
Delicious Turnip & Potato Curry 60
Devilled Potatoes. 62
Drumstick (Murunga) Curry 64
Green Beans And Carrot Curry 66
Green Beans In Sweet Aromatic Condiments 68
Leeks With Shredded Sweet Potatoes 70
Mixed Vegetable Curry In A Hurry! 71
Green Beans – With No Gas! 72
Lasagna Without Pasta! With Eggplant, Zucchini & Sweet Red Pepper. 74
Lentil Curry 76
Sautéed Broccoli, Perfumed With Aromatic Nutmeg 78
Sautéed Leek Greens 80
Steam Stir-fried Shredded Cabbage & Sweet Potato. 81
Potatoes For Brunch 82
Pumpkin Curry 84
Sautéed Long Beans (Mae-karal) (In Onions & Dried Shrimp) 86
Sweet 'N Sour Cabbage. 88
Sweet Potato & Zucchini Curry 90
Vegetable Stew 92

RICE & NOODLES

Citrus-flavoured Sweet Wild Rice 96
Fried Rice With A Twist! 98
Kiributh 100
Spaghetti With An Attitude! 103
Rice Vermicelli With Stir-fried Veggies 104

FISH CURRIES

Baked Sardine 108
Fish In Dark Tamarind Sauce 110
King-fish, Head & Tail Curried 112
Pan-fried Tilapia With Anise-scented Cannelloni Beans. 114
Prawn (Shrimp) Curry. 116
Quick 'N Easy Shrimp Preparation For Two! 118
Salmon Curry In A Hurry!. 120
Spicy King Fish Curry 122

MEAT CURRIES

Beef Curry In A Hurry!. 126
Beef Curry In Zucchini, Onions & Tomato Sauce. 128
Calf Liver With Sautéed Onions 130
Grandma's Famous Beefsteak 132
Ground Sirloin Curry In A Hurry! 134
Egg White Curry 136
Hamburgers With A Twist 137
Ma's Gourmet-flavoured Healthy Hamburgers 138
Ma's World-famous Chicken Curry!. 140
Veal Liver Curry 143

AN IMPROMPTU MEAL OF FOUR DISHES

ONE	Salmon Steaks 146
TWO	Roasted Potatoes & Butternut Squash 147
THREE	Kale 148
FOUR	Basmati, With Wild Rice 149

SAMBOLS

Carrot Sambol 152
Lunumiris Sambol 153
Okra Sambol. 154
Pol Sambol. 156
Seeni Sambol (Regular). 162
Seeni Sambol – With Sautéed Japanese Eggplants. 164

DESSERTS & TEA-TIME FAVOURITES

Banana Chocolate Chip Muffins 168
Paeni-pol 170
Sweet Crepes 171
Swarna's Carrot Cake – A Family Favourite 172
Yogurt In Kitul Paeni With A Twist 173

EASY HOME-MADE STOCKS

Beef Stock For Fried Rice 176
Chicken Stock For Fried Rice # 1 177
Chicken Stock For Fried Rice # 2 178

SPICES & COMBINATIONS FOR MAXIMUM FLAVOUR

Making Your Own Curry Powder 182
All-purpose Roasted Curry Powder 183
Basic Spice Condiments 184
Curry Powder For Vegetables 185
Easy To Make Curry Powder For Stuffings, Dips Or Soups 186
Garam Masala 187
Spice Mixture For Oven Fried New York Fries 188

Glossary 191
Availability 201

PREFACE

I learned to appreciate the different flavours, textures and tastes of food as a 5-year old sitting on my father's lap. At meal time, it was his routine to first feed the youngest one around. So when it was my turn, he would create, for his only girl among a bunch of 8 boys, a mouthful of food, each time adding different curries into the mix. My taste buds couldn't wait to savour each taste! He loved tasty food, and only the freshest of locally harvested ingredients.

My mother loved to put together meals with flavourful combinations. What goes with what was very important to her. And my aunt, my father's only sister, had a unique talent as well to come up with spice blends to enhance the natural flavour, be it veggies, fish or meat.

Living away from home, first in the US and then in Canada, I had to teach myself the art of cooking, never having stepped into mom's kitchen! I wanted to see taste, nutrition and colour in my dishes. Our two children from a very young age were exposed to international flavours, Sri Lankan ones being one of their favourites. I started creating recipes to approximate the tastes and aromas that my tongue still remembered from childhood through teenage years.

As our son and daughter grew up, they evolved into sophisticated food connoisseurs, placing ever more demands on my evolving culinary expertise. Their satisfied palates were inspirational. And it was their strong pleadings to put on paper my recipes that was the inspiration behind Cooking from the Heart. I give them a big hug for their encouraging feedback.

My husband totally believed in my recipes and the meal combinations I put together. While I would not see him until the food was on the table – he was my on-call sous-chef and an always dishwasher, he nevertheless ate with his appreciative eyes first.

But my heartfelt thanks go to him for a different reason as well. These recipes would not have left my warm kitchen and the notebook, and seen the light of day in print, if not for his persistent coaxing and the many hours spent at his computer, and in copy-editing. Thanks also for many of the pictures that adorn the pages of this work.

The spices and the condiments in the Recipes have been deliberately chosen for their intrinsic healing properties and tongue satisfying flavours. While all such flavour-enhancers are integral to a given curry, the 'hotness' of a spice may be modified to suit one's taste buds and culinary daring. The term 'spices' may conjure images of 'tongue-burning', but this is a sad misunderstanding. While some spices, like chillies, e.g., do indeed give your tongue a bite, many a spice simply adds flavour without the sting. Cinnamon, sweet and aromatic, but not hot, would be an example.

I hope you and your family will enjoy the many flavours that these loving spoonfuls from my family kitchen will give you as much as I have enjoyed creating them. Wherever health benefits are touched on, you should consult with your doctor, or better, nutritionist. For any unfamiliar ingredients, you may consult the Glossary.

I thank my niece Enoka de Silva with computer-related assistance. To Design Consultant Teri Watkins, Cassidy Taber for the layout, and all the other friendly members of the AuthorHouse team goes my thanks for facilitating access to this labour of love to a wider audience.

Swarna Sugunasiri
Toronto, Ontario, Canada
July 2008

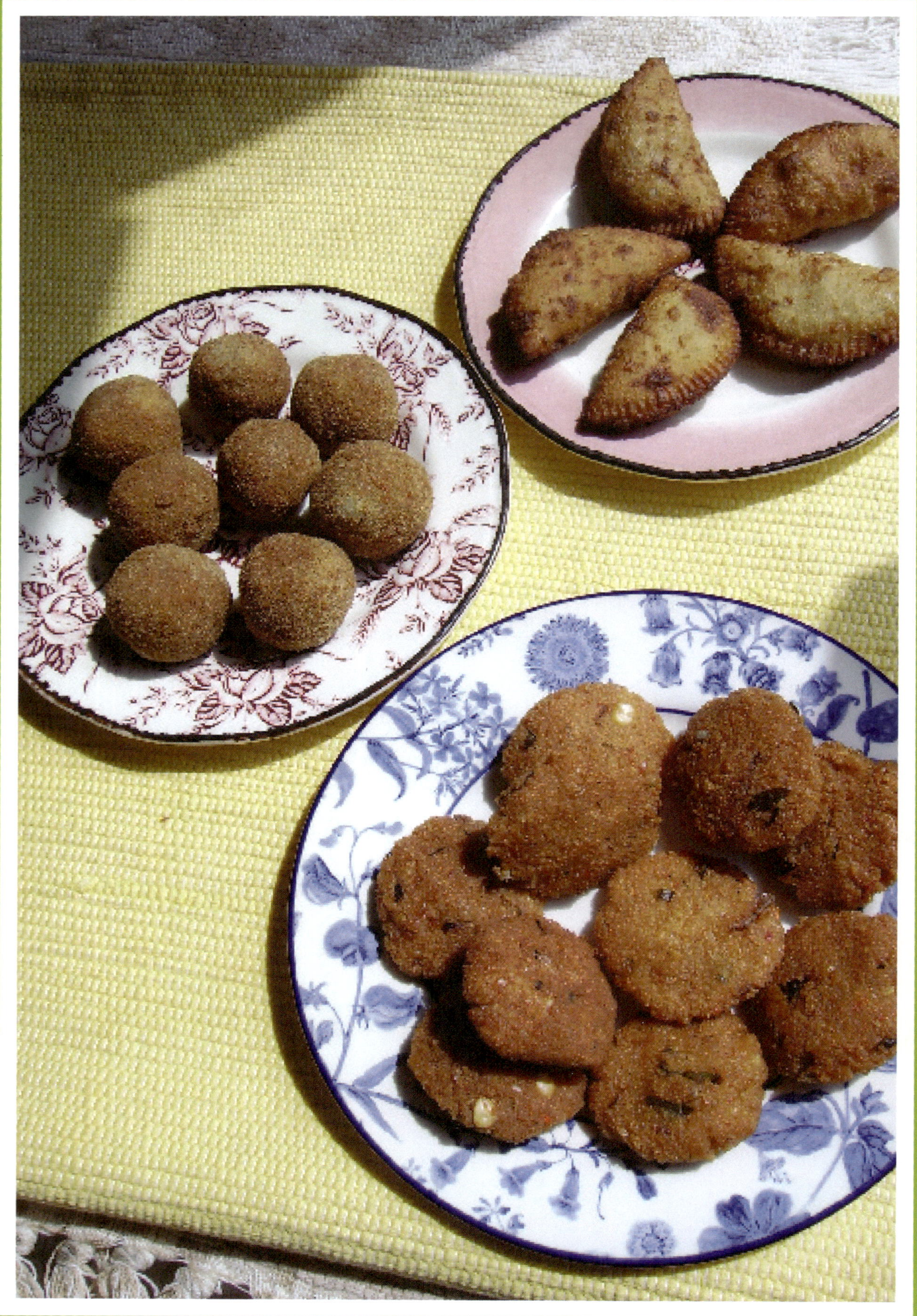

Savories

Beef Patties
Fish Cutlets
Lentil Fritters

BEEF PATTIES
Watch out! This is addictive!!

INGREDIENTS

2	potatoes	medium, cut into quarters
2 Tablespoons	vegetable oil	
1	onion	medium, finely chopped
½ lb	lean ground beef	
1 teaspoon	chillie powder	
1 teaspoon	black pepper	freshly ground
½ teaspoon	ground turmeric	
1 teaspoon	cumin	freshly ground
1 teaspoon	coriander	freshly ground
½ teaspoon	salt	
½ cup	leeks	chopped (white part only)
1 teaspoon	lime juice	
2 Tablespoons	spring onions	finely chopped (OR chives)
	Vegetable oil	(for deep frying)

NOTE

- You can substitute meat with canned or boiled mackerel or tuna for a different flavour.

PREPARATION

- Boil potatoes until soft.
- Drain water and let the potatoes dry and get fluffy in the same hot pan.
- Mash coarsely, and set aside.
- In a sauté pan, heat oil over medium high heat. Add the onions and cook until golden brown.
- Increase heat to high medium, add meat and brown it quickly, without covering.
- Add the rest of the ingredients except the lime juice and chives. Turn down the heat to low Mix well to combine meat with potatoes, spices and the vegetables.
- Cook for about 5 minutes at medium low heat.
- Add lime juice and chives. Check for seasoning. Turn off the heat & remove pan.

FOR PASTRY

INGREDIENTS

2 cups	all-purpose flour	
½ teaspoon	salt	
1/3 cup	butter or ghee	
½ cup	ice water	
½ teaspoon	anise seeds	coarsely minced
1	egg yolk	lightly beaten

PREPARATION

- Rub flour, salt and butter together. Add water gradually until mixture forms a dough.
- Knead for about 5 minutes. Press into a disc, cover with plastic wrap and place in the fridge for about 30 minutes to rest.
- Roll out the dough until about 1/8" thick.
- Cut roughly into about 4" circles. Place in a cookie sheet and cover with a tea towel to prevent the dough from getting dry.
- Take each pastry round and place about a Tablespoon of the meat filling in the centre, brush one end with egg yolk and fold pastry over. Press edge with a fork to seal.
- Line a baking sheet with parchment paper. Arrange patties in the baking sheet, keeping them apart.
- Leave in the fridge for about 20 minutes.
- Deep fry in batches, for about 5 minutes each batch, until golden brown.
- Drain on paper towel.

SERVING SUGGESTIONS

- As an appetizer.
- As a savoury snack with your afternoon tea.

FISH CUTLETS

A snack you can enjoy any time of the day!

"My family loves to snack on these before sitting down for the main meal. Sometimes we had cutlets with our afternoon tea."

INGREDIENTS

2 Tablespoons	vegetable oil	
1 sprig	curry leaves	
2	onions	medium, finely chopped
1	green chillie	seeded, & finely chopped
2 cans	tuna	drained & flaked
	(OR boiled mackerel)	
2	potatoes	medium, boiled & coarsely mashed
¼ teaspoon	turmeric	ground
1 teaspoon	cumin	ground
1 teaspoon	coriander	ground
	salt & pepper to taste	
1	lime	juiced
	bread crumbs	(for coating)
	vegetable oil	(for deep frying)

BATTER INGREDIENTS

1 cup	all-purpose flour
½ teaspoon	salt
½ teaspoon	pepper
½ cup	water

PREPARATION

- Heat the 2 Tablespoons of oil in a non-stick sauté pan over medium heat.
- Add curry leaves, onions, green chillies, cumin and coriander, and fry until lightly browned.
- Add drained tuna, and heat through for 2 minutes.
- Add mashed potato, and turmeric. Mix well.
- Season with salt, pepper and lime juice.

MAKING THE BATTER

- In a medium bowl, mix flour, salt and black pepper.
- Make a well in the centre and add enough water to make a thick dropping batter.
- Shape tuna mixture into small balls, dip in batter, coat in bread crumbs and leave in fridge for about ½ an hour.
- Take them out of t he fridge and deep fry until golden brown.

VARIATIONS

For tuna: lamb or extra lean ground beef could be substituted.

SERVING SUGGESTIONS

- As an appetizer.
- As an afternoon savoury snack.

Savories

LENTIL FRITTERS

Make sure that you make enough to share with neighbours. The wafting aroma is irresistible!

INGREDIENTS

2 cups	split peas (yellow)	
1	onion	medium, diced
1	green chillie	seeded & chopped
2 cloves	garlic	chopped
2 teaspoons	red chillie flakes	
4 to 6 Tablespoons	chickpea flour	(also called 'Besan flour')
1 teaspoon	salt	
½ cup	dried shrimp	soaked, washed & crushed
½ cup	warm water	
2 sprigs	curry leaves	snipped into pieces with scissors
	vegetable oil	(for frying)

PRE-PREPARATION

- Pick split peas for any specks of grit and stones.
- Wash and drain. Transfer into a big bowl and cover with cold water, let soak overnight, or at least for 6 hours.

PREPARATION

- Drain split peas and grind in a food processor in 2 batches.
- Add the first batch with all the ingredients except oil.
- Pulse blend until the mixture is combined, but still at a coarse consistency.
- Transfer the first batch into a bowl and add the second batch.
- Pulse blend until the mixture is crumbly.
- Mix well with the second batch.
- Add the chickpea flour and mix well.
- Rub your palms with vegetable oil.

- Take a small amount of the mixture, about the size of a golf ball, roll it into a ball, then press down into your cupped palm and press down to make them as thin as you can, without breaking them. [Thin fritters fry well and have a nice crunch when you bite into them.]
- Heat vegetable oil in a wok or deep fry pan at medium high heat.
- As you make them, lower them into the hot oil (using the slotted spoon) in small batches for about 4-5 minutes, until they are golden brown, keeping the heat at medium.

SERVING SUGGESTIONS

- As an appetizer.
- As a savoury snack with tea.

NOTE

They can be frozen for months. When you pull them out of the freezer, place them in a cookie sheet and heat them through in a toaster oven. They'll still be crunchy & delicious!

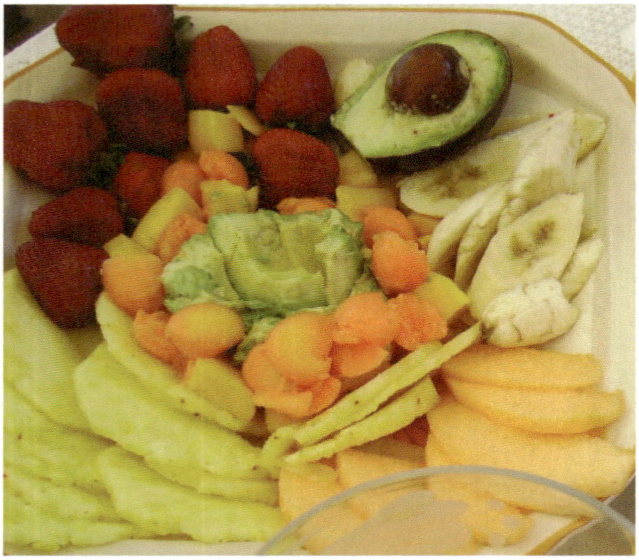
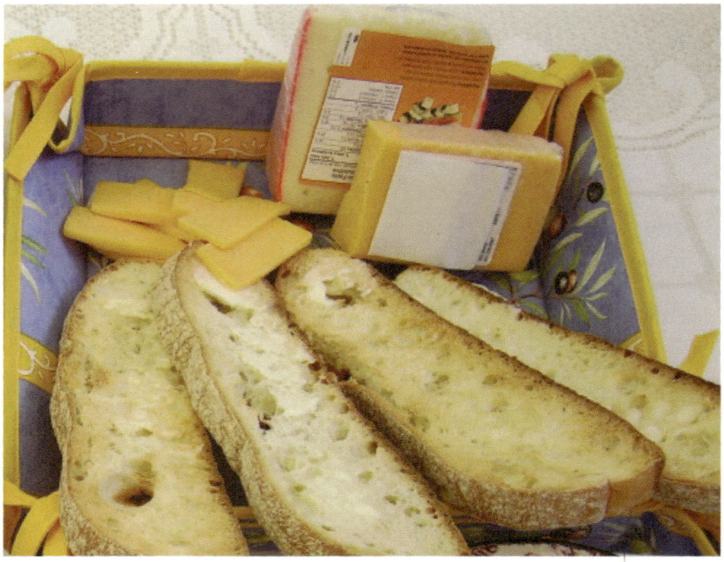
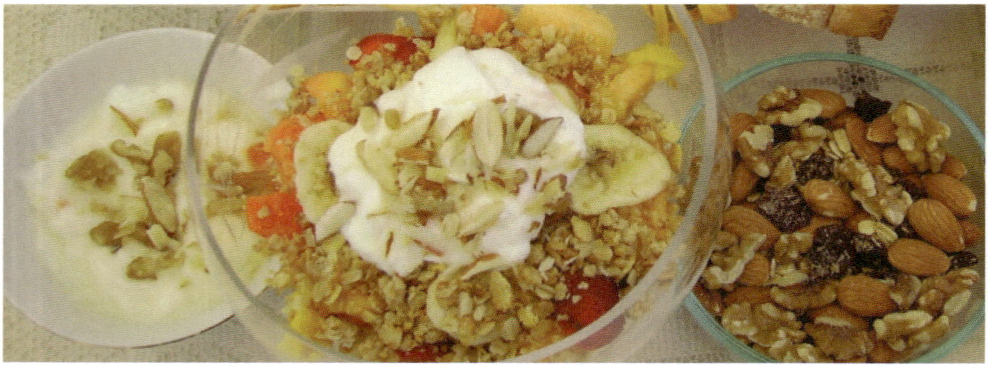
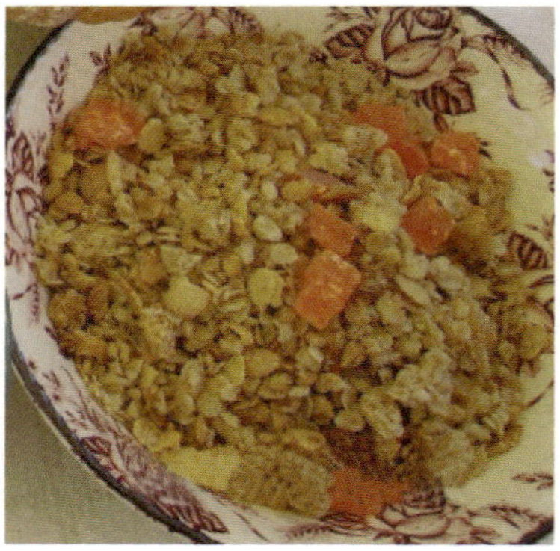
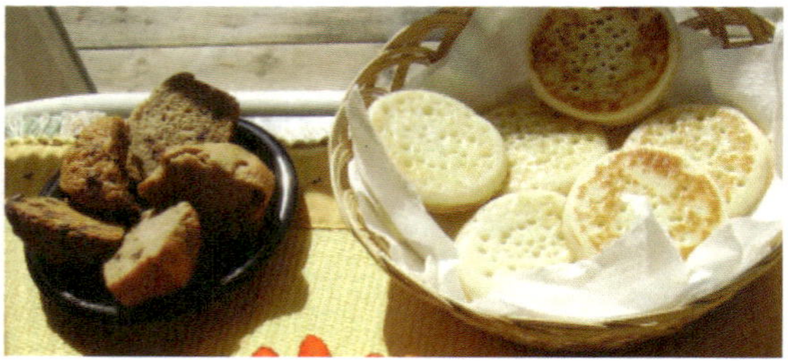
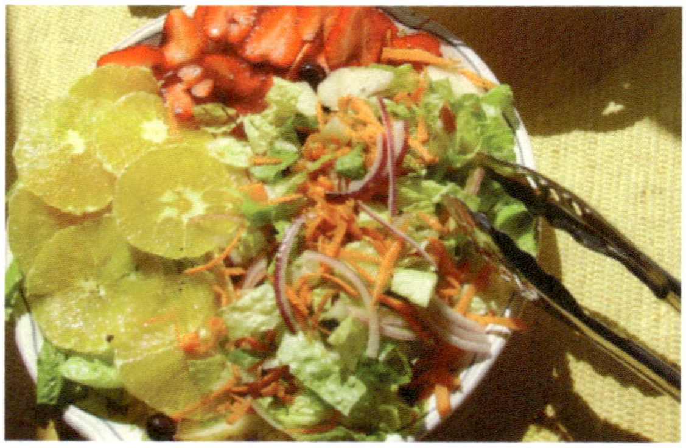
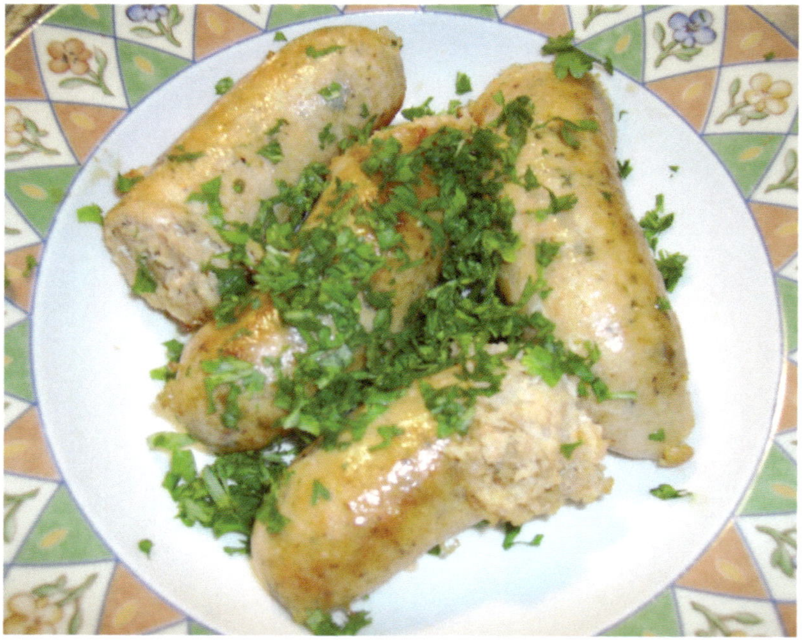

Brunch

Our Favourite Brunch Spread

3

ONE
OPENER

| 2-3 | juicy oranges | cut into thin wedges, unpeeled |

TWO
FRUIT, NUT N' YOGURT MELANGE

1	papaya	peeled & cut into bite size wedges
1	mango	peeled & cut into bite size wedges
2	avocados	scooped out & cut into bite size wedges
1	small cantaloupe	cut into bite size wedges
2 cups	sweet pineapple	chunks
1 cup	blueberries	
1 cup	hulled strawberries	
1 tub	plain vanilla yogurt	
½ cup	toasted walnut	
½ cup	toasted almonds	
1/3 cup	toasted sunflower seeds	
1/3 cup	toasted sesame seeds	

THREE
SAVORIES

6	multigrain bagels	halved and toasted
1 package	smoked salmon	
1	purple onion	thinly sliced
2-3 cups	button mushrooms (OR Cremini mushrooms)	thinly sliced and sautéed
1 pkg	cream cheese	at room temperature
6-8	fresh chorizo sausages*	split in half and cooked, and cut into bite-size pieces
5	medium onions	sliced coarsely
2 Tablespoons	Olive oil	to sauté the onions
1 Tablespoon	butter	to sauté the onions
8-10	savoury crepes OR crumpets	bought at the Supermarket OR Sri Lankan hoppers (home-made)**
6-8 pieces	home-baked carrot cake	(see Recipe in this book)
4	banana muffins	home-baked (see Recipe in this book), cut in halves

* to be bought at a Farmer's Market
** If you're lucky, you might be in a city where there are Sri Lankan caterers who will do the cooking in your own kitchen.

If not, here's how you may try your hand:

- Hopper Mix is readily available at Sri Lankan groceries.
- You may also get your special hopper pan (it looks like a miniature wok) while you're at it.
- You need at least two pans.
- The batter can be prepared (see below) and left in the refrigerator overnight.
- You need to have a couple of those special pans that you can buy at the same Sri Lankan grocery store.

Not only do they taste divine, it is also a fun activity to make them in your own kitchen. Try it, and you'll for sure, get hooked.

Brunch

FOUR
BASIC BATTER FOR HOPPERS

INGREDIENTS

1 lb.	white wheat flour	
16-24 ozs.	coconut milk	
1 pinch	salt	
1 pinch	sugar	
1 pinch	baking soda	
1 teaspoon	yeast	dissolved in 2 ozs. of tepid water.

PREPARATION

- Sieve the flour into a bowl, add salt, yeast and sugar, and mix enough water to make a thick dough. Set aside, to rise, for 2 to 3 hours.
- Gradually mix in the coconut milk, and leave for one hour or more to rise.
- Add the pinch of baking soda, mix well.
- Season a hopper pan with sesame oil.
- Heat the pan at medium high heat.
- Pour a spoonful of batter into the pan, pick it up (with gloves on) and tilt-circle it, as in making a crepe.
- Place the pan back right away. Cover with lid. Let cook for about 2 minutes in medium high heat. Watch for over-burn of the wafer thin crust forming all-around, leaving a thick crumpet base in the centre!
- Using a spatula, loosen the hopper crust carefully, and lift the hopper off the pan.

Now you're ready to enjoy it – hot, with any of the favourite savories, or with banana or a piece of jaggery (available at Sri Lankan stores) or a piece of dark chocolate. Voila!

TIP:

You may break an egg onto the centre crumpet for an **egg-hopper**, a Sri Lankan favourite.

FIVE
A FINAL TOUCH!

Flavoured tea or coffee (to suit each one's preference)

12

Our favorite brunch spread of fruits & nuts, yogurt, salad, toast/crumpets/muffins, & eggs, bacon & sausage

Brunch

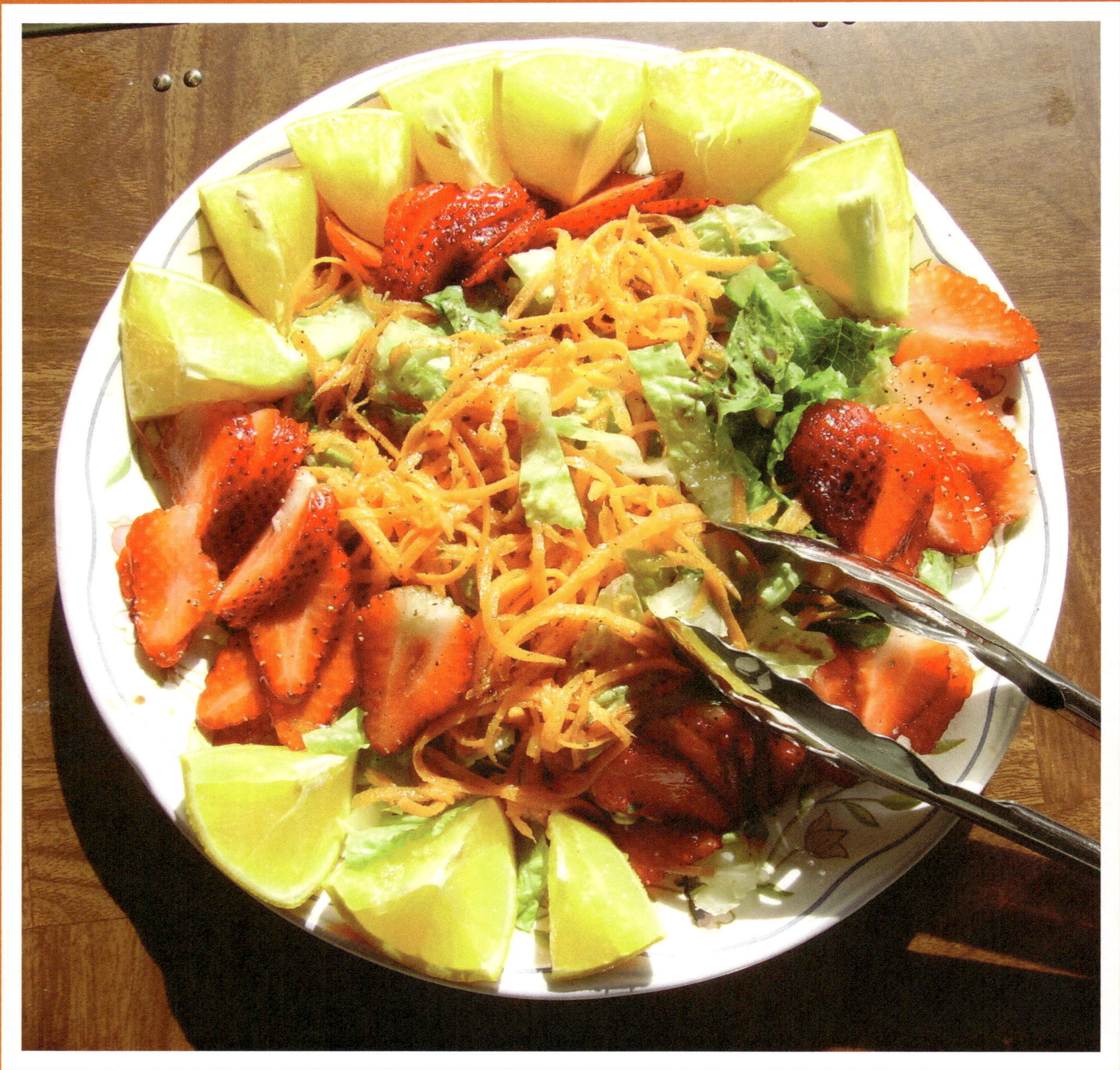

Fresh Salads

Colour & fresh ingredients are key in my salads.

LOW-FAT BUT CREAMY DRESSING
(FOR ALL SALADS)

INGREDIENTS

½ cup	plain NO-fat yogurt
¼ teaspoon	salt
¼ teaspoon	freshly ground black pepper
2 teaspoons	Dijon mustard
1 clove	minced garlic
2 teaspoons	extra virgin Olive oil
1 Tablespoon	freshly squeezed lemon juice
2 teaspoons	gourmet rice wine vinegar

PREPARATION

- In a glass measuring jar, combine minced garlic, Dijon mustard, salt & pepper.
- Add Olive oil & whisk until smooth.
- Add yogurt, lemon juice, & rice vinegar. Whisk until smooth & creamy.
- Refrigerate & use as needed.

HEALTH BENEFIT

Your liver will be thankful as it gets rejuvenated!

APPLE-TURNIP SALAD
Serves 4

INGREDIENTS

½	apple	green or red, cored, in match-stick cut
2	turnips	white, medium size tender, in match-stick cut
½	jicama	peeled, in match-stick cut
2 Tablespoons	pineapple	fresh, in match-stick cut
¼ teaspoon	sea salt	(optional)
½ teaspoon	fennel	seeds, ground
½ teaspoon	pepper	freshly ground black/white
1 teaspoon	lemon juice	
1 teaspoon	white sugar	

PREPARATION

Mix all ingredients in a colourful dish & serve as a side dish with roast pork, roast veal, roast chicken or baked fish.

HEALTH BENEFIT

Adds a good dose of potassium to your diet.

Salads

ASPARAGUS, GREEN BEANS, CARROT & BEET SALAD
Mouthwatering!

INGREDIENTS

½ lb	asparagus	blanched
½ lb.	green beans	blanched
4	carrots	medium, blanched
4-5	beets	medium, boiled or roasted
2	spring onions	sliced at an angle
¼ cup	sliced almonds	toasted
	salt & pepper	to taste

PREPARATION

- Wash the asparagus in cold water until the buds are grit-free Cut into 2" pieces.
- Wash & trim green beans, and cut in half.
- Wash, peel and cut carrots into three chunks each.
- Boil the beets in their skins, then peel off, and slice.
- Place cooked vegetables in a nice platter, and pour the dressing over.
- Garnish with the spring onions and the toasted almonds.

For added colour and flavour, you can add any cooked vegetable on hand, such as, cooked but crispy cauliflower.

COLESLAW WITH ANISE & DRY MUSTARD POWDER

INGREDIENTS

½	cabbage	savoy or regular, medium, finely shredded.
½	anise	fresh bulb, shredded finely
1	carrot	finely shredded
1 teaspoon	ginger	fresh, grated
1 teaspoon	mustard powder	freshly ground
1 teaspoon	black / white pepper	freshly ground
1 teaspoon	kosher salt	
1 Tablespoon	coarse sea salt	(for rinsing cabbage)
1 Tablespoon	lemon juice	freshly squeezed
1 Tablespoon	Olive oil	extra virgin
1 Tablespoon	rice wine vinegar	

PREPARATION

- Put shredded cabbage in a bowl & stir with the sea salt. Set aside for twenty minutes.
- Assemble the shredded carrot & anise in another bowl & set aside.
- Make the dressing by mixing the Olive oil, rice wine vinegar, lemon juice, salt & pepper. Check & adjust seasonings.
- Rinse the cabbage in cold water & squeeze gently. Add to the carrot & anise & mix well.
- Pour the dressing over the vegetables. Mix well. Taste & adjust seasonings. Cover with a plastic wrap & refrigerate.

SERVING SUGGESTINGS

- With baked chicken & home made New York Fries.
- Fish fried in tampura batter, oven fried potatoes & steamed green beans.

Savoy cabbage gives a nice tender crunch!

Salads

CUCUMBER & YOGURT SALAD
A great side dish for a meal with rice & chicken!

INGREDIENTS

1	cucumber	medium, thinly sliced
2	shallots	finely chopped
¼ teaspoon	salt	
¼ teaspoon	pepper	
¼ teaspoon	ginger	freshly grated
1 teaspoon	lime juice	freshly squeezed
1	green onion	finely chopped
1/3 cup	yogurt	plain no-fat
1	green chillie	finely chopped
1 teaspoon	honey	

PREPARATION

- Combine the salad ingredients in a glass bowl. Taste for flavour. Add more salt or pepper if needed.
- Serve with rice, couscous or bulgar.

DEEP-FRIED ANCHOVY (DRIED SPRATS) SALAD

INGREDIENTS

1 packet	dried sprats (anchovy)	
1	onion, white or purple, medium	sliced
½	lime	freshly squeezed
1	green chillie	fresh, finely sliced
	(OR jalapeno pepper)	
¼ teaspoon	black pepper	freshly ground
1 cup	Canola oil	
	(OR vegetable oil)	

PREPARATION

- Soak sprats in cold water for about half an hour. Rinse with several changes of water {5-8} times. Spread on paper towels & pat dry.
- Heat oil in a wok or a fry pan at high heat. Drop a clove of garlic with skin on to check if the oil is hot enough. {It is a quick method of flavouring the oil, too}.
- Now put dried sprats into the hot oil. Stir occasionally.
- Turn the heat down to low medium.
- When the sprats are golden brown & crispy drain on paper towels.
- Set aside.
- In a medium bowl, assemble the sliced onion & green chillies.
- Now add the fried sprats, black pepper & lime juice. Mix & serve.
  [Thinly sliced fresh tomatoes could also be added just before serving for added depth of flavour & colour.]

DEEP-FRIED BITTERGOURD SALAD
A mouthwatering side dish to a rice & curry meal!

INGREDIENTS

3-4	bittergourds	medium, dark green variety
1	onion	large, finely sliced
½	a lime	
½ teaspoon	black pepper	
½ teaspoon	salt	(if needed)
2 Tablespoons	sea salt	(for the brine)
1 cup	Canola oil	(for deep frying)
1	green chillie	finely diced {optional}

PREPARATION

- Wash & dry bittergourds.
- Slice finely. Put in a medium bowl & add enough lukewarm water to cover the sliced bittergourds.
- Add the 2 tablespoons of sea salt & mix well. Cover & let stand for 20 –30 minutes .
- Heat oil in a wok or a deep sauce pan.
- Squeeze gourds thoroughly & dry in paper towels. Add to the hot oil in small batches & fry until golden brown.
- Set aside on paper towels.
- Put fried gourds in a nice dish. Add the finely sliced onions & green chillies.
- Squeeze the lime juice over the fried gourds & the thinly cut onions. Mix well. Serve immediately.

SERVING SUGGESTIONS

- As a side dish for a rice n' curry meal that includes a 'long lentil curry' (Recipe in this collection) (meaning lentils cooked in A lot of gravy) and sardine cooked in tamarind sauce (Recipe in this collection).

SOME SUGGESTED VARIATIONS

If desired , the thinly sliced onions, too, could be deep fried before adding to the fried gourds. But fry the onions separately & blot off the oil using paper towels.

Add finely chipped Maldive fish (see Glossary) to imbue another level of authentic flavour.

This is a mouthwatering side dish to a rice & curry meal. Those who hate eating bitter gourds will turn instant converts, I am sure.

HEALTH TIP

An excellent vegetable to keep your blood sugar level normal.

To make it a more healthful side dish, follow all the steps given except for deep frying. Serve it as a raw salad.

Salads

ICEBERG LETTUCE SALAD #1
Low Fat, Quick & Easy

INGREDIENTS

½ head	Iceberg Lettuce	shredded
1 pinch	sea salt	
¼ teaspoon	pepper	white or black
1 teaspoon	Olive oil	extra virgin
2 Tablespoons	rice wine vinegar	gourmet
¼	English cucumber	cut into thin sticks
1	tomato	ripe, cut into bite size wedges
1 Tablespoon	Greek feta cheese	

PREPARATION

- Spread shredded lettuce in a nice platter.
- Add cucumber sticks & tomatoes.
- Sprinkle salt & pepper. Drizzle the Olive oil & sprinkle rice vinegar, making sure to mix well with the lettuce.
- Crumble feta cheese over the lettuce.
- Taste & add more vinegar, if needed.

SOME SUGGESTED VARIATIONS

1 cup baby spinach
½ a sweet bell pepper, julienned
1 medium carrot grated into matchsticks
½ a red onion, julienned
A few calamata Olives, chopped

ICEBERG LETTUCE SALAD #2

INGREDIENTS

½ head	iceberg lettuce	shredded
1 pinch	sea salt	
¼ teaspoon	Black/white pepper	
½ teaspoon	crushed chillies	
1 teaspoon	extra virgin Olive oil	
1 Tablespoon	extra virgin Olive oil	(for sautéing)
1 Tablespoon	Light soy sauce	
2 Tablespoons	Gourmet rice vinegar	
1	zucchini	small, julienned
1	sweet bell pepper	julienned
1	purple onion	medium, thinly sliced
2 cloves	garlic	finely chopped
1 hunk	feta cheese	

PREPARATION

- Assemble the following ingredients in a medium bowl. shredded lettuce with a sprinkling of salt & pepper & one teaspoon of Olive oil . Add the rice vinegar.
- Set aside.
- On the stove heat up a skillet with the tablespoon of Olive oil .
- Add onion & then the garlic.
- Add zucchini & bell pepper & stir well.
- Add the crushed chillies & the salt & pepper.
- Add soy sauce & the remaining rice vinegar. Stir until the vegetables begin to wilt.
- Remove from heat & add to the lettuce salad. Garnish with feta cheese {optional}.

Salads

ORANGE PERFUMED WARM COUSCOUS SALAD
It's simply delicious!

INGREDIENTS

1 cup	couscous	fine or medium
1 teaspoon	cumin seeds	roasted
1 teaspoon	coriander seeds	freshly ground
½ teaspoon	kosher salt	
½ teaspoon	black pepper	
½ teaspoon	crushed chillies	(increase to your liking)
1	orange zest	
2 teaspoons	Canola oil or Olive oil	
1 Tablespoon	unsalted butter or ghee	
½	a purple onion	thinly sliced
2 Tablespoons	parsley	chopped
	(OR cilantro or mint)	
1 cup	sweet peas	frozen or fresh
½ cup	pine nuts or walnuts	roasted
½ cup	hot water or chicken stock	
2 Tablespoons	rice wine vinegar	
1 wedge	fresh lemon	
4 thin slices	smoked Italian sausage	{optional}
1	plum tomato	seeded & diced finely
1	small zucchini	diced finely
1	carrot	grated at medium size

PREPARATION

- Pour a cup of couscous into a medium bowl.
- Pour about ½ a cup of hot water or stock over the couscous. Add enough liquid only to cover the couscous. Cover & set aside. (In five minutes the couscous will be ready to be fluffed with a fork.)
- Heat oil in a sauté pan at medium high heat.
- Add oil & butter.
- When heated, add cumin seeds.
- When the aroma begins to waft into your face, add diced onions & stir.
- Now add crushed chillies & the coriander powder. Stir well.
- Add zucchini, tomatoes & parsley.

- Add the orange zest & mix well.
- Add the frozen peas & continue to stir cook.
- Add carrots & nuts, stir well.
- Add diced Italian sausage & mix well.
- Now uncover the couscous & fluff with a fork.
- Sprinkle the rice wine vinegar& fluff again.
- Sprinkle some parsley or mint over the couscous.
- Fold in gently the mixture in the sauté pan with couscous.

SERVING SUGGESTIONS

- Serve with plain yogurt or with fruit bottom yogurt. It's simply delicious.

SOURCE OF INSPIRATION FOR THIS RECIPE

The texture of couscous reminded me of a fabulous breakfast we had had at the Galle Face Hotel in Colombo, Sri Lanka, when we were on holidays in 2000. The texture of couscous is identical to the texture of pittu – a rice flour based preparation steamed just like couscous. Except that the pittu is steamed in a traditional cylindrical mould & cut into serving size pieces. At the hotel, pittu was served* with a delicious king fish curry, cooked in a mildly spicy coconut gravy. There was a spicy red mutton curry, too, in addition to the traditional lunumiris (red chillie sauce) (Recipe in this collection) with lots of Maldive Fish (a fish condiment used only in Sri Lanka. See Glossary).

- You may order this on the internet, now in many a western city. Try Australia, Canada and UK in particular.

Salads

PARSLEY SALAD

INGREDIENTS

1	curly parsley	bunch, finely chopped
2	shallots	large, finely chopped
1 pinch	salt	
¼ teaspoon	black/white pepper	
3 Tablespoons	coconut	freshly grated {optional}
1 Tablespoon	Maldive fish	finely chopped {optional}
1 Tablespoon	lime juice	freshly squeezed
1 clove	garlic	finely minced

PREPARATION

- Mix the ingredients in a medium size bowl.
- Mix the salad well using your hands (not the mixer or the food processor).
- Taste & add more lime juice if needed.

NOTE

Create a **spicier** version of the salad by adding a tender green chillie chopped finely.

SERVING SUGGESTIONS

- Parsley salad can be the accompanying salad for a dinner menu that includes steamed rice, lentil curry and baked or fried fish, or beef or pork curry.

HEALTH TIP

This salad is heart healthy and has a good potassium–sodium balance.

ROMAINE LETTUCE SALAD WITH HONEY GARLIC DRESSING

INGREDIENTS

½ head	romaine lettuce	washed, spin dried & cut into bite size pieces
½ cup	red cabbage	finely shredded
2	tomatoes	medium, cut into bite size wedges
1	carrot	medium, finely julienned
½	a sweet bell pepper	cut in thin strips
¼	anise	finely shredded

DRESSING

2 cloves	garlic	finely chopped
¼ teaspoon	salt	
¼ teaspoon	pepper	
2 Tablespoons	lemon juice	
2 Tablespoons	orange juice	
¼ cup	extra virgin Olive oil	
1 Tablespoon	honey	
½ teaspoon	mustard powder	freshly ground

PREPARATION

- In a small bowl, whisk together all of the above ingredients for the dressing.
- Mix the salad ingredients in another medium size bowl. Toss well.
- Sprinkle the dressing & toss again.

Voila! It's ready.

Salads

SALAD FOR TWO - WITH PEARS, ANISE, TOMATO & ONIONS (red n' white)

INGREDIENTS

½	pear	thinly sliced
¼	anise	bulb, thinly sliced
½	purple onion	small, thinly sliced
½	Vidalia onion	thinly sliced
1 Tablespoon	lemon juice	
1	tomato	vine-ripe, cut in wedges
1 Tablespoon	red wine vinegar	
1 Tablespoon	Olive oil	
½	baby cucumber	thinly sliced
	salt & pepper to taste	
1 pinch	crushed red chillies	

PREPARATION

- Put sliced onions in a small salad bowl & lightly mix with fingers to brake up & mix the onions.
- Add sliced anise & mix well.
- Add wedges of tomato & the thin strips of cucumber.
- Arrange the first & the last two ingredients on top of the salad.
- Mix lemon juice, salt & pepper, wine vinegar & the Olive oil .
- Sprinkle over the salad

SERVING SUGGESTIONS

Serve with a pasta meal.

HEALTH BENEFIT

In addition to the crunch, this salad works wonders in your digestive tracks. Enjoy!

TOMATO & PURPLE ONION SALAD
A very refreshing side salad!

INGREDIENTS

4	tomatoes	ripe medium, cut in wedges
1	purple onion	medium, finely sliced
¼ teaspoon	salt	
¼ teaspoon	pepper	
1 teaspoon	crushed chillies	
1 Tablespoon	Maldive fish	finely chopped (optional)
1 teaspoon	extra virgin Olive oil	(optional)
	lime juice to taste	

PREPARATION

- Wash tomatoes well.
- Cut into small wedges. Arrange in a medium size bowl.
- Add the onions, salt & pepper, crushed chillies, Maldive fish & lime juice.
- Now add the Olive oil & mix well.

NOTE

This is a very refreshing side salad for a main meal of rice & curry.

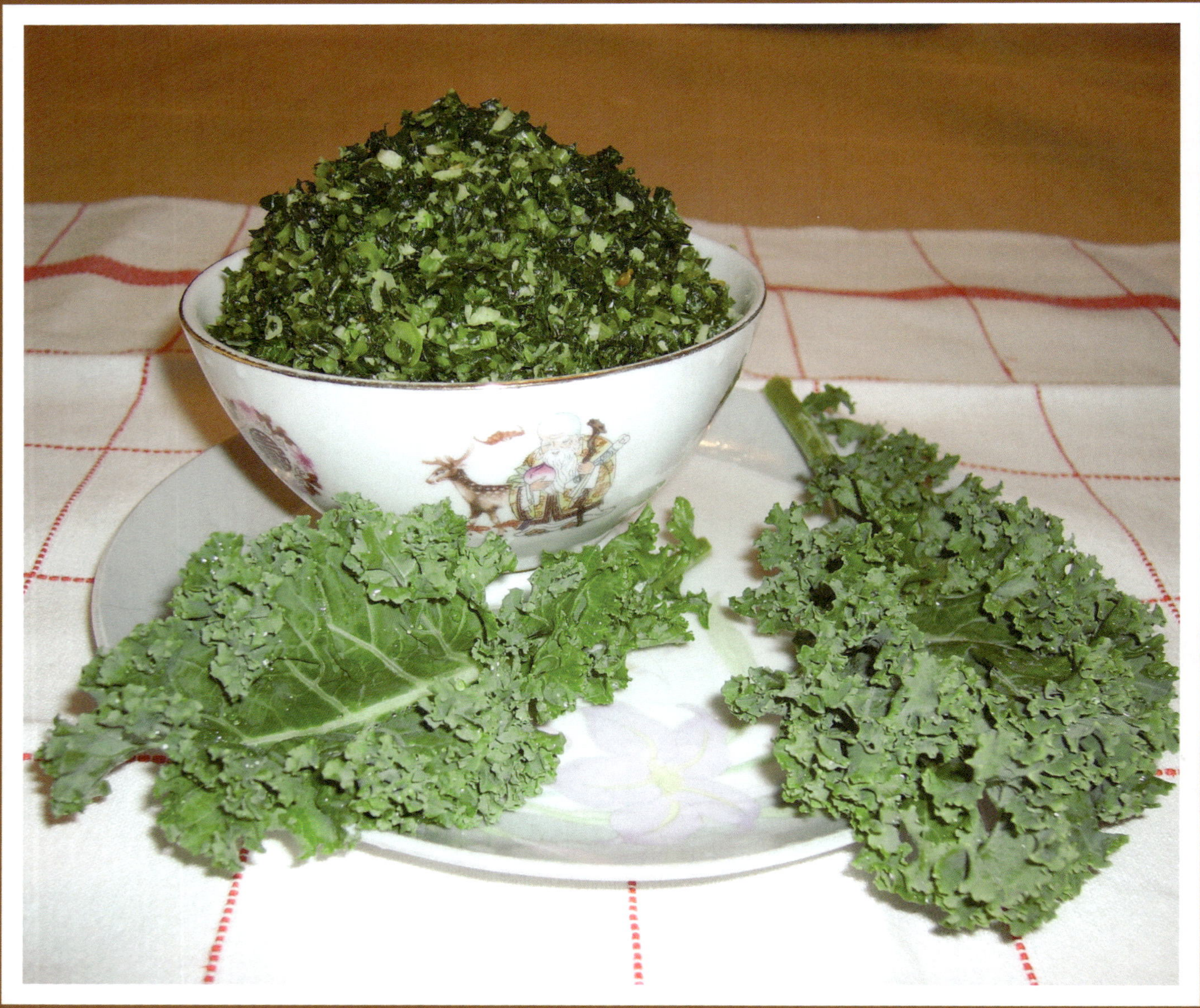

Mallung: Dry-Cooked Salads

['Mal-' pronounced like 'mat', /u/ in '–lung' (NOT as in English 'lung' but) as in 'soon', only shorter, as in 'put']

Mallung, or dry-cooked salads, are something unique to Sinhalese (Sri Lankan) cuisine. Every garden has a spot where one or two edible plants are grown alongside the fence or around the family well or a vine that climbs up our temple-flower (araliya) tree or a breadfruit (del) tree.

Fresh green and tender leaves are harvested, washed and cut into fine shreds. Then they're smeared with a sprinkling of salt water, and dry-cooked in medium heat, but without covering the pan. In the last step, some freshly grated coconut is mixed with the cooked greens for added flavour.

While this technique of cooking ensures retention of most of its nutrients and the bright green colour, it also adds a veggie accompaniment with a different texture to be mixed with rice, the staple diet in this part of the world..

Enjoy the following four Mallung!
1. Cabbage Mallung
2. Collard Mallung
3. Kale Mallung
4. Polos-Gaeta (Young Jack-Fruit) Mallung

CABBAGE MALLUNG, USING SAVOY CABBAGE
A nice balance of flavour & texture to a rice & curry meal!

INGREDIENTS

1	cabbage	medium, finely chopped
½ cup	coconut	freshly grated
2 teaspoons	mustard powder	freshly ground
1 teaspoon	cumin	freshly ground
2 teaspoons	coriander powder	freshly ground
½ teaspoon	turmeric	
2 teaspoons	black pepper	freshly ground
5-6 cloves	garlic	finely chopped
2 teaspoons	ginger	freshly grated
1 two-inch piece	cinnamon	
1 Tablespoon	Olive oil or Canola oil	
½ cup	water	
1 pinch	nutmeg	freshly grated
1 Tablespoon	lemon juice (OR rice wine vinegar)	fresh

PREPARATION

- Heat oil in a wide sauté pan or a Dutch Oven.
- Add chopped cabbage & cinnamon & stir well.
- Add water, lemon or vinegar. Stir & cover.
- Turn down heat to high medium.
- Meanwhile, combine coconut, mustard powder, turmeric, cumin, coriander, garlic, ginger, salt & pepper in a small food processor (or, in a stone mortar & pestle if you can find one).

- While the food processor is going, check if the cabbage is wilted & nearly cooked. Give a good stir.
- Add the processed condiments & stir well.
- Add the pinch of nutmeg & stir again.
- Cook uncovered & check for taste.
- Adjust heat to make sure that the cabbage is not soggy, nor too dry. It should just be fluffy when you stir with a fork.
- At the very last stage, you can turn off the heat & leave the pot on the stove until you remove the cabbage into a dish.

NOTE

Cabbage cooked this way stays fresh in the fridge for up to 4-5 days. This dish can be prepared ahead & frozen if needed. If frozen, put back in the fridge a day ahead. To freeze the cooked cabbage divide into portions, put in freezer bags spread & flatten the cabbage & lay them flat in the freezer.

This dish gives a nice balance of flavour & texture to a rice & curry meal. It could be served with curried lamb, beef, chicken or fish.

SOURCE OF INSPIRATION FOR THIS RECIPE

This recipe was written down on March 12, 2000. I prepared this dish 10 days ahead of time, for our daughter Tamara's Call to the Bar Celebration. I wrote it down while listening to the Titanic, a gift from her.

COLLARD MALLUNG
The meditative chef-knifing is therapeutic!

INGREDIENTS

1 bunch	collard leaves	washed & dried
½ teaspoon	lime juice	freshly squeezed
¼ teaspoon	sea salt	
1 teaspoon	crushed chillie flakes	
3 Tablespoons	coconut (OR from your freezer, not desiccated coconuts)	grated fresh*
3 big cloves	garlic	finely chopped
1 teaspoon	mustard powder	
1 pinch	nutmeg	freshly grated
2 teaspoons	Olive oil	

*see Glossary

PREPARATION

- Wash collards in lots of cold water. Drain & pat dry with a tea towel or paper towels.
- Pile 4-5 collard leaves & roll into a tight bundle crosswise. Cut in half.
- Now hold both bundles together & cut into very fine shreds*. Use a Chef's knife.
- Put the shredded collards in a medium bowl.
- Put a sauté pan on medium high heat. Add the Olive oil.
- Add the chopped garlic & stir.
- Now add the collards & stir well. Keep stirring.
- Add salt & the chillie flakes.
- Turn down the heat to a medium low. Keep stirring & do not cover.
- When the greens begin to get dry, add the grated coconuts, mustard powder & the pinch of nutmeg.

- Turn off the heat.
- Remove the pan from the heat , add the lime juice & stir well before serving into a wide dish. Spread out the cooked greens to help the greens to keep its vibrant colour.

* Modern day cooking aficionados have a fancy term for this: cheffanade. But this was how my mom always cut green leaves picked from her backyard for those tasty & nutritious Mallung she used to make for us.

HEALTH TIP

If you want to retain the authentic taste & nutritious value of the greens, resist the temptation to use the Food Processor, hand-cutting will give you far superior results.

Believe you me, the meditative chef-knifing is therapeutic, too.

SERVING SUGGESTIONS

- With Rice & Curry
- With Short Pastas like Penne
- With Meat & Potatoes

KALE MALLUNG

INGREDIENTS

1 half a bunch	Kale	
4 cloves	garlic	minced
¼ teaspoon	kosher salt	
½ teaspoon	chillie flakes	
½ teaspoon	mustard powder	
4 Tablespoons	coconut (OR desiccated unsweetened coconut)	freshly grated*
1 grate	nutmeg	
2 teaspoons	Olive oil	

* Saving tip: When you happen to get a good coconut, grate it (Instructions in this book), divide into portions & freeze in freezer bags. Thaw & use. It will be just as fresh!

PRE-PREPARATION

- Wash kale in cold water and put in a colander to drain.
- While the kale is drying, mince the garlic.
- Break off the end stems of kale and set aside.
- Using a paper towel or a clean kitchen towel, dry little bundles of kale leaves.
- Take each little bundle, roll it like a cigar and, using a sharp knife, shred as finely as possible.
- When you finish shredding the leaves, gather the end stems, bruise them with the back of the knife and mince the stalks. Set aside separately.

PREPARATION

- Heat a wide sauté pan at medium high and add the Olive oil.
- As the oil gets heated, add crushed chillies and garlic, and stir.
- After a few seconds, add the stalk part of the kale and stir cook for about 10 seconds, then add the rest of the kale and continue to stir.
- Keep stirring until the kale is reduced in a mound and has turned to a vibrant green.
- Mix the salt, chillie flakes and the mustard powder with the coconut, and add to the greens in the pan and mix well.
- Add a grate of fresh nutmeg and continue to stir.
- When the greens are dried and light but still has the vibrant green colour, turn off the heat, take it off the burner and transfer to serving platter immediately.

SERVING SUGGESTIONS

- As a side vegetable with steamed rice, string hoppers or noodles.

My recipes retain colour and nutrients.

පොලොස් ගැට මැල්ලුම

POLOS-GAETA (YOUNG JACK-FRUIT) MALLUNG

Have an exotic Sinhalese (Sri Lankan) meal right at home!

['o' in 'polos' (both) is pronounced NOT as in the game 'polo' but as in the English term 'apropos']

INGREDIENTS

Don't be discouraged by the long list of ingredients. This is a fast & easy recipe.

1 can	young jack fruit	rinsed, drained, squeezed & finely chopped
½ cup	grated coconut*	
1 teaspoon	mustard powder	
½ teaspoon	black pepper	
½ teaspoon	salt	(add more if needed)
2	green chillies	finely chopped
1 teaspoon	crushed chillies	
1 teaspoon	cumin powder	
1 teaspoon	coriander powder	
½ teaspoon	turmeric	
5 thin slices	ginger	fresh, finely chopped
2 teaspoons	Maldive fish chips	fine
1	onion	medium, finely chopped
3-4 cloves	garlic	finely chopped
1 Tablespoon	Olive oil (OR Canola oil)	
1 teaspoon	lime juice	fresh

- When you happen to get a good coconut, grate it (see Instructions in this book), divide into portions & freeze in freezer bags. Thaw & use. It will be just as fresh!

PREPARATION

- Rinse, drain & squeeze out the Jack Fruit pieces.
- Pat dry & chop finely.
- Mix cumin, coriander, mustard powder & turmeric with the grated coconut.
- Heat oil & sauté garlic, onion, ginger & chillies.
- Add Jack Fruit crumbs & stir well.
- Turn down the heat to medium. Add salt, pepper, Maldive fish & crushed chillies. Stir well.
- When the condiments are cooked & blended well with the Jack Fruit, taste to check the seasoning & add the lime juice to enhance flavour.
- Turn off the heat & give it a final stir.

NOTE

Canned Jack Fruit is available in Thai, Vietnamese or Sri Lankan stores. It is an inexpensive grocery item that can wait on your pantry shelf until needed.

SERVING SUGGESTIONS

Serve this side dish with steamed rice & the following curries:

- Chicken or beef curry
- Dhal {lentil} curry
- Parsley salad
- Pappadum (see Glossary)

Bon appetite!

Mallung

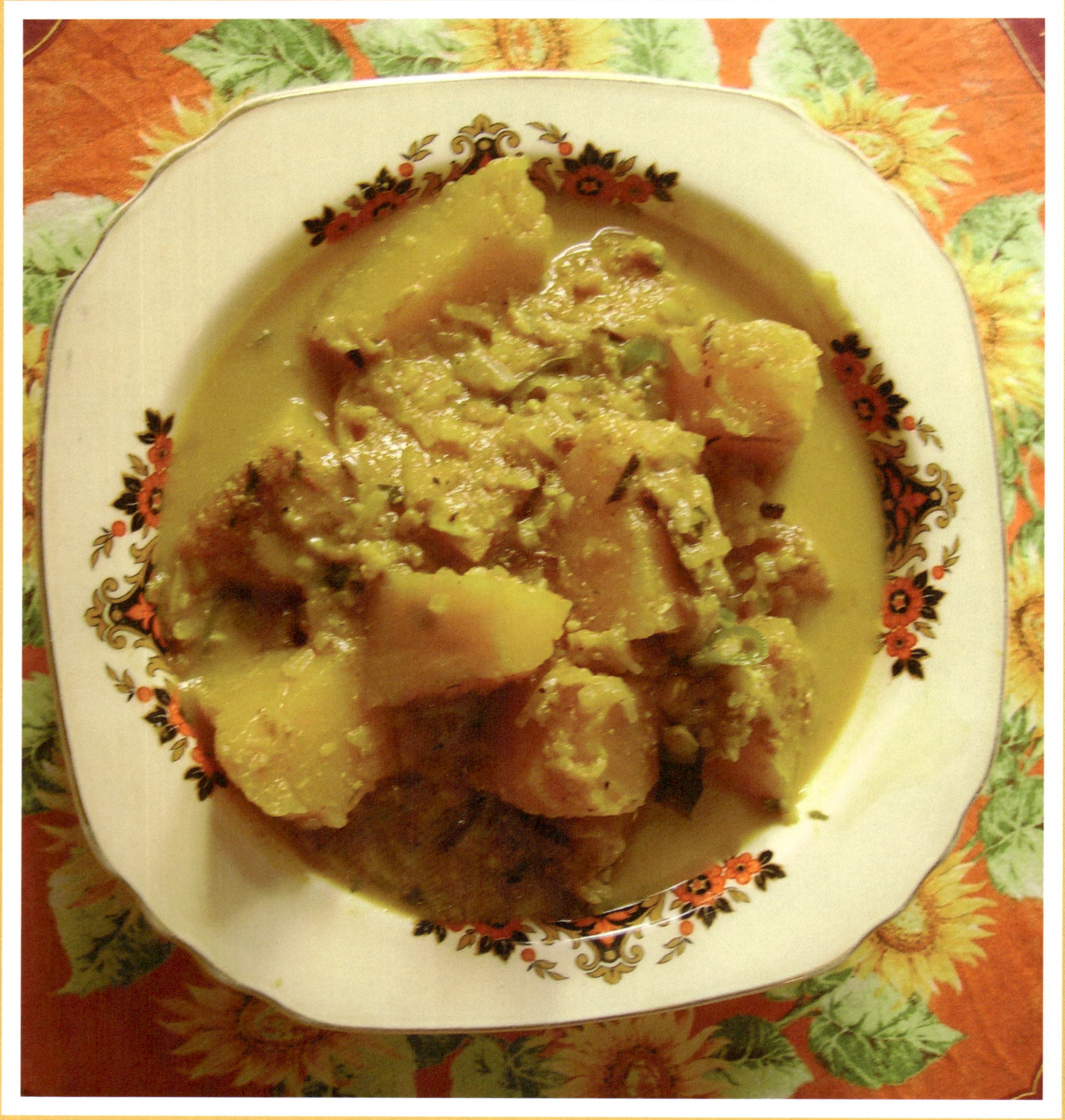

Vegetable Curries

ASH PLANTAIN CURRY
BLACK EYE PEAS WITH MIXED VEGETABLES
CADJU [CASHEW] CURRY
CARAMALIZED FENNEL & ONION , IN TAMARIND SAUCE
CUCUMBER WHITE CURRY
CURRIED BLACKBEANS WITH LEFTOVER ROASTED VEGETABLES!
MIXED CAPSICUM CHILLIES CURRIED
CURRIED EGGPLANT, WITH CHICKPEAS & SWEET BELL PEPPER
CURRIED EGGPLANT, WITH PEPPERS & ONIONS
CURRIED EGGPLANTS, CUBERNALE PEPPERS AND ONIONS
DELICIOUS TURNIP & POTATO CURRY
DEVILLED POTATOES
DRUMSTICK (MURUNGA) CURRY
GREEN BEANS AND CARROT CURRY
GREEN BEANS IN SWEET AROMATIC CONDIMENTS
LEEKS WITH SHREDDED SWEET POTATOES
MIXED VEGETABLE CURRY IN A HURRY!
GREEN BEANS – WITH NO GAS!
LASAGNA WITHOUT PASTA! WITH EGGPLANT, ZUCCHINI & SWEET RED PEPPER
LENTIL CURRY
SAUTÉED BROCCOLI, PERFUMED WITH AROMATIC NUTMEG
SAUTEED LEEK GREENS
STEAM STIR-FRIED SHREDDED CABBAGE & SWEET POTATO
POTATOES FOR BRUNCH
PUMPKIN CURRY
SAUTÉED LONG BEANS (MAE-KARAL) (IN ONIONS & DRIED SHRIMP)
SWEET 'N SOUR CABBAGE
SWEET POTATO & ZUCCHINI CURRY
VEGETABLE STEW

ASH PLANTAIN* CURRY
An exotic meal, without ever having to step out of your house!

INGREDIENTS

5-7	ash plantains	fresh-looking, peeled & sliced in ½" piece
2	green chillies (OR 1 jalapeno pepper)	diced
1 sprig	curry leaves*	
1 teaspoon	fenugreek	
¼ teaspoon	turmeric powder	
2 teaspoons	Maldive fish*	
1 teaspoon	cumin powder	
1 teaspoon	coriander powder	freshly ground
2 teaspoons	salt	
1 teaspoon	black pepper	
1	onion	medium, diced
2 1" pieces	cinnamon	
1 cup	coconut milk*	diluted
1 teaspoon	Olive oil	(OR Canola oil)
¼ cup	vegetable broth	(OR hot water)
1 teaspoon	curry powder	roasted

* Available in Sri Lankan or Indian grocery stores.

PREPARATION

- Peel, wash & slice the plantains.
- Put in a bowl, & sprinkle turmeric powder over the plantain.
- Add coriander & cumin powder & mix well.
- Soak fenugreek seeds in hot water.
- Heat oil in a medium saucepan, & add the drained fenugreek seeds; turn down heat.
- Add curry leaves & cinnamon, salt, black pepper, green chillies, garlic & onions, & stir until lightly brown.
- Add plantains & mix well; keep the heat at medium-low.
- Add quarter cup of vegetable broth or hot water; cover & let cook, stirring occasionally.
- When the plantains are almost cooked, add the coconut milk, & stir well.
- Add the Maldive fish; cover, & let cook for 5 minutes
- When the coconut milk is cooked & blended into a nice, thick gravy, sprinkle the roasted curry powder over the plantains.
- Take the pan off the heat, and transfer into a serving dish.

SERVING SUGGESTIONS

- Steamed rice, with a red curry of kingfish, tuna, halibut or mullet, a green maellung (e.g., kale, collard or cabbage) & pappadum (see Glossary).
- Serve immediately.

You now have an exotic meal, without ever having to step out of your house!

BLACK EYE PEAS WITH MIXED VEGETABLES
A delicious & nutritious vegetarian dish!

INGREDIENTS

2 cups	black-eye peas	dried
2	plum tomatoes	seeded & diced
2	onions	medium, diced
1	carrot	organic, grated coarsely
4 cloves	garlic	finely chopped
1 teaspoon	cumin seeds	roasted
1 teaspoon	black mustard seeds	
1 teaspoon	coriander	freshly ground
1 teaspoon	crushed chillies	
1	lemon zest	
1 teaspoon	kosher salt or sea salt	
1 teaspoon	black pepper	
3 slices	ginger	julienned
1 Tablespoon	Olive oil or Canola oil	
1 sprig	curry leaves (OR 1 bay leaf)	

PREPARATION

- Wash black eye peas in two changes of water.
- Transfer the peas into a medium size saucepan. Fill it with cold water just above the peas.
- Add two bay leaves & cover the pot leaving it slightly ajar.
- Cook at high heat until the water boils down & peas are cooked to a nice soft texture.
- Transfer the cooked peas into a bowl.
- Put the pot back on the burner & add Olive oil.
- Add cumin seeds, chopped garlic, curry leaves, & mustard seeds.
- When the mustard seeds begin to pop, add onions, ginger, carrot & tomatoes. Stir.
- Add salt & pepper & crushed chillies & let cook for about two minutes.
- Stir well & add the cooked peas & mix well again. Let the peas get flavoured in the condiments & vegetables in low heat.
- In about five minutes, turn off the heat. Stir in a tablespoon of lemon juice or freshly squeezed carrot juice. The peas will have the consistency of a vegetable stew.

SERVING SUGGESTIONS

- on a bun – instead of a hamburger
- on a bed of couscous pilaf.
- as a side dish for a rice & curry meal.

CADJU [CASHEW] CURRY

INGREDIENTS

½ lb	cadju nuts	dried
1 teaspoon	fenugreek seeds	
2 teaspoons	coriander powder	
1 teaspoon	cumin powder	
2-3 teaspoons	chillie powder	(adjust to your taste)
¼ teaspoon	turmeric powder	
½ teaspoon	baking soda	
1-1½ teaspoons	sea salt	
1 Tablespoon	Olive oil	
1	onion	medium, thinly sliced
1 cup	coconut milk	
1 1" piece	cinnamon	
1 sprig	curry leaves	
2 cloves		
1 pod	cardamom	

PREPARATION

- Boil some water in a pot, or microwave in a glass jar.
- Pour water over the cadju nuts in a bowl to cover the cadju nuts.
- Add baking soda, & let soak for 1 hour.
- Transfer cadju nuts & the water into a sauce pan, & boil covered for about 4-5 minutes, until cadju nuts are tender but not too soft.
- Drain & wash well in cold water.
- Heat the oil in a sauce pan, add curry leaves & onions, & fry till onions are light brown.
- Add the cadju nuts mixed well with all the condiments & salt. Let cook covered for 5-10 minutes.
- Add the coconut milk. Bring to boil, cover, & let simmer till done.

NOTE

- Omit chillie powder if a white curry is desired. Add 2-3 diced green chillies instead.
- Sprinkle a teaspoon of roasted curry powder for an authentic flavour.

SERVING SUGGESTIONS

- As a side dish for a meal that includes flavoured rice or fried rice.
- As a much coveted, and very portable, pot-luck dish for an alms-giving for Buddhist sangha (ordained men & women).

Vegetable Curries

CARAMALIZED FENNEL & ONION, IN TAMARIND SAUCE

INGREDIENTS

1 small bulb	fennel	thinly sliced
1	onion	medium, thinly sliced
2 Tablespoons	shrimp	small dried
2 cloves	garlic	thinly sliced
1 Tablespoon	sherry vinegar	
1 sprig	curry leaves*	
1 Tablespoon	lemon zest	(optional: orange zest)
1 teaspoon	crushed chillies	
½ teaspoon	black pepper	freshly ground
1 teaspoon	curry powder	roasted (home made)**
1 teaspoon	sea salt (OR 1 ½ teaspoon kosher salt)	
1 Tablespoon	Canola oil (OR Olive oil)	
2 teaspoons	tamarind paste	diluted in a tablespoon of hot water

* available in Sri Lankan or Indian stores
** See Recipe in this book.

PREPARATION

- Heat a sauté pan at medium heat.
- Add oil, then garlic & curry leaves. Stir & let it turn aromatic.
- Add shrimp & stir.
- Add fennel & mix well.
- Add sliced onions & stir well to combine the condiments.
- Add salt, lemon & orange rind & crushed chillies. Turn heat down & continue to cook.
- Add the tamarind sauce & mix well with the rest of the ingredients. Let cook at low heat, covered.
- Taste for seasoning. To enhance the sweet & sour flavour, add one teaspoon of white sugar. Taste & add another ½ teaspoon of sugar if necessary.

SERVING SUGGESTIONS

- as a side dish with steamed rice or string hoppers
- on a sandwich along with other sandwich stuffings

NOTE

This preparation could be preserved in the refrigerator for up to two weeks.

A TIME SAVING TIP

An efficient way to get instant citrus zest is to zest fresh lemons, limes, & oranges before using them. Wrap in plastic food wrap, put in a zip-lock bag & keep in the freezer. They are ready when you need them.

Vegetable Curries

CUCUMBER WHITE CURRY

You can really go to town with this curry!

NOTE
This is essentially a gravy dish for a rice and curry meal. It goes well with string hoppers and a spicy fish preparation. When the spicy fish creates heat in the mouth, the cucumber curry will provide a fresh, cooling sensation!

INGREDIENTS

2	field cucumbers	peeled, seeded, quartered lengthwise & cut into 1 inch thick wedges
1	onion	medium, diced
3 cloves	garlic	sliced
1 1" sliced	ginger	minced
2 2" pieces	rumpé*	
2	Kaffir lime leaves*	torn into big pieces
1 2" piece	cinnamon	
1 sprig	curry leaves	
1 teaspoon	Dijon or grainy mustard	
2 teaspoons	fenugreek seed	soaked in water
2 teaspoons	coriander powder	
2 teaspoons	cumin powder	
1 teaspoon	fennel powder	
¼ teaspoon	whole pepper corn	
¼ teaspoon	turmeric	
1½ teaspoon	sea salt	
2 teaspoons	Olive oil	
1 Tablespoon	Maldive fish chips	
¼ cup	water	
½ cup	cream of mushroom soup	
1 cup	coconut milk**	(using coconut powder or canned coconut milk)

* Available in Asian groceries.
** See Instructions in this book.

PREPARATION

- Place saucepan on medium-high; add oil.
- When oil is heated, add curry leaves, garlic, ginger & drained fenugreek seeds. Cook stirring.
- Add all other ingredients, except cream of mushroom & coconut milk. Cover & let cook for about 5 minutes , or until cucumber is half-done.
- Dilute cream of mushroom with coconut milk, & heat through in the microwave.
- Add warmed cream of mushroom & milk mixture. Stir well. Cover partially, & let curry come to a soft boil.
- Taste for seasoning. Turn off the heat.
- For depth of flavour, add a squirt of lime juice. Keep partially covered, until ready to serve.

SERVING SUGGESTIONS

This is essentially a gravy dish.

- With string-hoppers.
- With naan (Indian flat bread) or roti

I like to serve this in the following combination:

- Steamed Basmati   or fried rice.
- sautéed long beans.
- Kingfish in dark or red spicy sauce.
- Pappadums for the crunch.
- Kale or collard Mallung, to round up the health benefits.

HEALTH BENEFIT

Cucumber, mixed with mushroom sauce, is
full of essential vitamins and minerals.

Vegetable Curries

CURRIED BLACKBEANS WITH LEFTOVER ROASTED VEGETABLES!

INGREDIENTS

1 14 oz. can	organic black bean	drained & rinsed well
½	onion	diced
1	carrot	diced*
1	celery stalk	diced
1 slice	ginger	minced
1 Tablespoon	parsley	chopped
	(OR mint if available)	
½ teaspoon	kosher salt	
½ teaspoon	black pepper	freshly ground
1 teaspoon	coriander powder	roasted
1 teaspoon	cumin powder	roasted
½ teaspoon	turmeric	
2 teaspoons	Canola or Olive oil	
2 cloves	garlic	minced
½ cup	warm water	

* I used a few pieces of leftover butternut squash

PREPARATION

- Heat sauté pan, medium high; add oil.
- When oil is hot, add onion, garlic & minced ginger. Cook stirring.
- Add diced vegetables; stir well.
- Add tomatoes, & stir well. Add beans, & stir well.
- Turn down heat to medium-low.
- Add coriander, cumin, back pepper, salt & turmeric. Cook stirring.
- Add water, stir & let cook covered for 1 to 2 minutes .
- Turn off heat, & sprinkle the chopped herbs over the beans.

SERVING SUGGESTIONS

- We had a tasty roti meal with this one!
- Try it inside a crusty Italian bun; or with naan or warm multigrain bread.

MIXED CAPSICUM CHILLIES CURRIED

INGREDIENTS

6 to 8	Capsicum chillies: sweet banana peppers, cubernale peppers & green ancho peppers	
2	medium onions	sliced
1 teaspoon	coriander powder	
1 teaspoon	crushed chillies	
1 teaspoon	roasted curry powder	
1 teaspoon	roasted fennel seeds	
2 teaspoons	cumin powder	
2 teaspoons	lemon or lime juice	
2 Tablespoons	Olive oil	
2 Tablespoons	medium sized dried shrimp (OR Maldive fish)	
2 cloves	garlic	sliced
1 2" piece	cinnamon	
¼ cup	vegetable broth, chicken stock, coconut milk (OR water)	

PREPARATION

- Wash & seed the peppers.
- Cut into 1/8 inch rings. Set aside.
- Add oil into a heated sauté pan at medium high.
- Fry onions & garlic. Keep stirring.
- Add peppers & stir well to coat all pieces in oil. Add spices, & mix well. Cover & let cook for about 2 minutes.
- Uncover, add the milk, broth or water, & stir well. Let cook covered for another 3 to 4 minutes.
- Uncover, sprinkle lemon or lime juice & stir well. Taste for seasoning.
- Turn off the heat.
- Transfer into a platter when you're ready to serve.

SERVING SUGGESTIONS

- Side dish for a rice & curry meal.
- With String hoppers or noodles.
- As a layer of stuffing for a multi-layered crusty bun.
- A flavourful stuffing in a wrap sandwich. Dot it with goat cheese for added flavour

Vegetable Curries

CURRIED EGGPLANT, WITH CHICKPEAS & SWEET BELL PEPPER

INGREDIENTS

1	eggplant (purple)	medium, cut in 2" wedges
1	sweet bell pepper	diced
2 stalks	celery	diced
1 28 oz can	chickpeas	rinsed & drained
1 teaspoon	kosher salt	
1 teaspoon	black pepper	freshly ground
1 teaspoon	coriander powder	
1 teaspoon	cumin powder	
½ teaspoon	turmeric powder	
1 teaspoon	fennel powder	freshly ground
1 2" piece	cinnamon	
½ teaspoon	ground mustard	
2 cloves	garlic	thinly sliced
3 Tablespoons	Olive oil	
1	onion	medium, diced
¼ cup	flat-leaf parsley	finely chopped
½ cup	tomato juice	
½ cup	water (OR vegetable OR low sodium chicken broth)	
½ teaspoon	chillie powder	
1 Tablespoon	small shrimp	dried

PREPARATION

- Heat a sauté pan at medium high.
- Add the Olive oil.
- When the oil is hot, add diced onion and garlic. Stir well.
- Add the shrimp. Stir.
- Add the diced vegetables and cook stirring.
- Add the spices. Mix well to coat each piece of vegetable well.
- Add tomato juice and the broth. Mix well, and let cook at medium low heat for 6 to 10 minutes.

SERVING SUGGESTIONS

- With steamed rice as a side dish.
- Mixed with couscous.
- With noodles or spaghetti

HEALTH BENEFIT

This is a meal full of cholesterol busting soluble fibre, potassium and a good amount of protein.

Vegetable Curries

CURRIED EGGPLANT, WITH PEPPERS & ONIONS

INGREDIENTS

2 to 3	eggplants (Japanese)
	(OR 1 small purple eggplant)
4 to 5	cubernale peppers
	(OR sweet banana peppers)
1	big Spanish onion or white onion
1 teaspoon	cumin seed
1 teaspoon	mustard powder
1 teaspoon	salt
1 teaspoon	pepper
1 teaspoon	crushed chillie
¼ teaspoon	turmeric
1 sprig	curry leaves
2-3 pieces	rumpé*
1	green cardamom bruised
2 Tablespoons	Canola oil
1 Tablespoon	extra-virgin Olive oil
¼ cup	tiny dried shrimp

* Available in Sri Lankan or Asian grocery stores.

PREPARATION

- Wash & dry the vegetables well.
- Cut in half the eggplant lengthwise, then in half again lengthwise, then into wedges 1/8" inch thick.
- Cut in half the peppers lengthwise, then in half again lengthwise, then into wedges 1" inch thick.
- Slice the Spanish onion lengthwise.
- Heat a wide non-stick sauté pan at medium-high; add the Canola oil.
- When the oil is hot, add the cumin seed & crushed chillie.
- Place eggplant wedges in the pan in one layer (try not to overlap).
- After a minute or two, turn over the wedges, & turn down the heat to medium. Let it cook uncovered for 5 minutes.
- Turn over again, making sure every piece is cooked in oil.
- Continue the process until the wedges are wilted & golden.
- Transfer the eggplant wedges on to a plate; set aside.
- Put back the pan on the stove, add the onions & peppers; cook stirring, for about 3 minutes.
- Cover, let cook for another minute or two.
- Uncover, & sprinkle about 2 Tablespoons of warm water or warm broth.
- Stir the vegetables, cover & let cook.
- After 2 or 3 minutes, add turmeric, curry leaves, rumpé, cardamom, salt, pepper & the crushed chillie.
- Sprinkle the Olive oil, & stir well. Allow the vegetables to cook, with the lid slightly ajar.
- When the vegetables are wilted, add the eggplants & mix well.
- Turn down heat, & let the vegetables get nicely wilted & blended together.

SERVING SUGGESTIONS

- Serve as a side-dish for a rice 'n curry meal or as a sandwich stuffing using Italian bread rolls.
- As a sandwich stuffing, using crusty bread rolls or multi-grain baguette.

Vegetable Curries

CURRRIED EGGPLANTS, CUBERNALE PEPPERS AND ONIONS

INGREDIENTS

2	Japanese eggplants	cut in half
	(OR 1 purple eggplant)	
4–5	cubernale peppers	cut
	(OR sweet banana peppers)	
1	big Spanish onion	cut
1 teaspoon	cumin seeds	
1 teaspoon	mustard powder	
½ teaspoon	salt	
½ teaspoon	pepper	
1 teaspoon	crushed red pepper	(optional)
¼ teaspoon	turmeric powder	
1 sprig	curry leaves	
2-3 1" pieces	rumpé*	
1	green cardamom	bruised
2 Tablespoons	Canola oil	
1 Tablespoon	Olive oil	extra virgin
¼ cup	dried shrimp	tiny
2 Tablespoons	hot water (OR chicken broth)	

* Available in Sri Lankan or Asian grocery stores.

PRE-PREPARATION

- Wash and dry the vegetables well.
- Starting with the eggplant, cut first in half, lengthwise, in half again, and then in strips of 1/8" thick.
- Then taking the pepper, cut first in half, lengthwise, and then into thick 1" strips.
- Lastly, cut onions into strips lengthwise.

PREPARATION

- Heat a wide non-stick sauté pan.
- Add Canola oil.
- When oil is nice and hot, add cumin seeds and crushed chillies.
- Place eggplant strips in one layer. Try not to overlap.
- After a minute or two, turn them over. Turn down the heat to medium and let cook uncovered.

- After another 5 minutes, turn over the eggplant again, making sure every piece is cooked in oil.
- Continue the process until the eggplants are wilted and golden. Transfer the eggplant into a plate and set aside.
- Put the pan back on the stove and add the onions and peppers. Cook stirring for about 3 minutes.
- Then cover with a lid and let cook for another minute or two.
- Uncover, and sprinkle about 2 Tablespoons of hot water or chicken broth. Stir the
  Vegetables, cover and let cook.
- After another 2 minutes, add the turmeric, curry leaves, rumpé, cardamom, salt & pepper and the tiny dried shrimp.
- Add the Olive oil and stir well. Let the vegetable cook well with the lid ajar.
- When they're wilted, add the eggplants and mix all the vegetables until they're nicely combined.
- Turn down the heat and let the vegetables get nicely wilted and blended.

SERVING SUGGESTIONS

- As a side dish for a rice & curry meal.
- As a sandwich stuffing for crusty Italian bread rolls.

HEALTH NOTE

This dish is not only nutritionally packed, but the eggplants, with its soluble fibre, also act as a cholesterol buster.

Vegetable Curries

DELICIOUS TURNIP & POTATO CURRY

INGREDIENTS

2	Chinese turnips	fresh & tender, sliced 1/8" thick
1	Yukon Gold potato (OR 3 to 4 small red-skin potatoes)	large, sliced 1/8" thick
1	onion	medium, diced
1 teaspoon	fennel powder	freshly ground
1 teaspoon	mustard powder	freshly ground
2 teaspoons	coriander powder	roasted
1 teaspoon	cumin powder	roasted
1 teaspoon	sea-salt (OR kosher-salt)	
1 teaspoon	black pepper	
½ teaspoon	turmeric powder	
½ teaspoon	fenugreek	roasted
½ teaspoon	whole cumin	
1 Tablespoon	dried small shrimp (OR Maldive fish*)	
1	green chillie (OR jalapeno pepper)	sliced
½ cup	vegetable stock (OR chicken stock)	
¼ cup	2% milk	
1 1" piece	cinnamon	
¼ teaspoon	chillie powder	
1 Tablespoon	Olive oil	

* Available in Sri Lankan grocery stores.

PREPARATION

- Heat Olive oil in a medium saucepan at medium heat.
- Add the diced onion and let it sweat.
- Add fenugreek seeds, cumin seeds and the dried shrimp. Stir.
- Add the cut vegetables and mix well.
- Add the spices, & mix well to coat each piece with the spices.
- Add the stock and the green chillies or jalapeno. Cover and let cook 2 to 3 minutes .
- When the vegetables are almost cooked, add the milk, stir well and turn down the heat.
- After about 2 minutes , taste for doneness and seasoning. It should turn out to be a dish with a thick gravy.

SERVING SUGGESTIONS

- Delicious with oven fried chicken and garlic toast as a side!

Vegetable Curries

DEVILLED POTATOES
An all-time Sri Lankan favourite!

This is an all-time favourite of Sri Lankan rice-lovers. Over the years, I have eaten devilled potatoes done by many a cook. But, my mom's devilled potatoes beat them all by far. Now, my family savours this dish with a vengeance!

This is a combination of dishes that my mother used to serve us. Instead of 'red chicken curry', she made a king fish curry. And she made a delicious 'kos mallung' (Jack Fruit) to go with it. It was wonderfully satisfying!

INGREDIENTS

1 lb	potatoes (my favourite is Yukon Gold)	
1 sprig	curry leaves	
½ teaspoon	turmeric	
2 Tablespoons	Maldive fish or tiny dried shrimp	
2	onions	medium, thinly sliced
2 cloves	garlic, sliced	
1 teaspoon	sea salt	
4 Tablespoons	Canola oil	
2 1" pieces	cinnamon	
2 teaspoons	chillie powder	
1 teaspoon	crushed chillies (if you like it spicy)	
2 teaspoons	sweet paprika	

PREPARATION

- Wash potatoes, & in a pot, boil the potatoes unpeeled.
- Drain the water & put potatoes back into the pot
- Turn off the heat; put saucepan on the burner. (This is done to allow potatoes to become dry & fluffy.)
- Peel, & cut potatoes into bite-size pieces.
- Put in a dry bowl. Add salt, turmeric, garlic, chillie powder, crushed chillie & Maldive fish. Mix well.
- Heat oil at medium-high in a wide shallow sauté pan.
- Add curry leaves & sliced onion (If using dried shrimp, add it now.)
- Fry for a few seconds. Add potatoes, & mix well with the roasted condiments. Make sure the pieces are in the pan in one layer. (This helps every piece to get crusted.)
- Cook uncovered for a minute or two. DO NOT stir during this period, but let the potatoes get crusty in the roasting condiments. Let cook for 2 minutes , & then turn over the pieces. (If the pan is too dry, add another sliced onion. Pour another Tablespoon of vegetable oil over the onion, & give it a stir. Cook covered for another 2 minutes .)
- Uncover, turn over the potatoes, & turn down the heat to low. Let the potatoes get crusty & devilled.
- When all pieces are covered with a brown, delicious crust, give it a squirt of lemon juice.
- Check for seasoning. Turn off the heat, but leave the pan on the stove.

SERVING SUGGESTIONS

Perfect, & colourful, with -
- steamed rice
- murunga cooked in a white gravy (see Recipe in this collection)
- red chicken curry
- carrot sambol (see Recipe in this collection).

Vegetable Curries

DRUMSTICK (MURUNGA) CURRY

(/u/ in 'murunga' is pronounced NOT as in English 'rung' but as in 'rune', only shorter, as in 'put']
An ideal companion for rice or string hoppers!

INGREDIENTS

1 lb	drumsticks	peeled & washed, & cut into 4" pieces
3 1" pieces	rumpé*	
2 1" pieces	cinnamon	
1 cup	coconut milk	(from coconut powder)**
	(OR ½ can canned coconut milk (unsweetened))***	
1 Tablespoon	vegetable oil	
½ teaspoon	turmeric	
1 sprig	curry leaves	
1 teaspoon	chillie powder	
2 teaspoons	cumin powder	
2 teaspoons	coriander powder	
1 teaspoon	fenugreek	(soaked in warm water)
1	onion	medium, diced
1 teaspoon	roasted fennel powder	
2 cloves	garlic	minced
2 teaspoons	salt	
1 Tablespoon	Maldive fish chips	
½ cup	warm water	

* Available at Chinese, Indian or Sri Lankan stores.
** Available in packets (that includes instructions) at Sri Lankan stores.
*** Available at any major grocery store.

PREPARATION

- Cut both ends of drumstick, peel fibrous skin (with a vegetable peeler) & cut each drumstick into 4" pieces. Wash in cold water, & set aside.
- Heal oil in a medium saucepan @ medium-high.
- Add mustard, fenugreek, garlic, curry leaves & onion. Stir well.
- Add coriander, cumin, fennel, chillie (powder), cinnamon & Maldive fish. Stir well.
- After 3 minutes, add drumstick, turmeric & salt.

- Add warm water, cover & cook for about 4 minutes.
- Uncover, when you begin to get the cooked aroma of drumstick, add coconut milk, & stir again.
- Cover partially & let curry come to a soft boil.
- Uncover, & stir until the gravy is smooth. Check for seasoning. Now the curry is ready to be served.

Fresh Murunga   Prepped Fresh Murunga

NOTE

Rice in Sri Lanka always loves the company of a long gravy for smooth sailing. This dish is an ideal candidate for the honour!

This is considered a delicacy by my children. They love to suck on the drumstick and scrape in with their teeth every bit of the delicate flesh, flavoured with mild curry. They enjoy it best with string hoppers* than with rice. Meat or fish prepared in a spicy dark sauce goes well with the murunga curry.

* Available in Sri Lankan restaurants, or are made to order in homes.

Murunga Curry

Vegetable Curries

GREEN BEANS AND CARROT CURRY

INGREDIENTS

½ lb	green beans	tender & fresh, blanched
1 stick	carrot	cut in 2" logs; then cut into thin strips,
	blanched	
2 teaspoons	cumin powder	
2 teaspoons	coriander powder	
¼ teaspoon	turmeric powder	
1 teaspoon	kosher salt	
1 teaspoon	black pepper	
1 teaspoon	crushed chillies	
1 sprig	curry leaves	
1	onion	small, sliced
2 cloves	garlic	minced
2 slices	ginger	minced
2 Tablespoons	Olive oil	
¼ cup	boiled water (from blanching beans & carrots)	
	Ketchup for flavour	

PREPARATION

- Boil water in a deep saucepan.
- Wash and clean green beans, and cut in half.
- Blanch in boiling water, until dark green, and tender.
- Drain immediately, and immerse in cold water.
- Do the same with the cut carrot sticks.
- Heat oil in a non-stick pan, and add the garlic, ginger, onions & curry leaves.
- Add salt & paper, and crushed chillies.
- Cook stirring at medium heat.
- Add the drained carrots & beans and the spices. Cook stirring. Do not cover.
- Add water from the blanching pot and stir well.
- Taste for seasoning.
- Add about 3 squirts of ketchup and give a good stirring.
- Transfer into a serving platter.

SERVING SUGGESTIONS

- As a side dish for rice n' curry meals.
- As a vegetable accompaniment for a meal of roasted meat or baked fish.

Sautéed Greens with freshly grated carrot.

Asparagus is a substitute for green beans.

Vegetable Curries

GREEN BEANS IN SWEET AROMATIC CONDIMENTS

INGREDIENTS

1½ lbs.	green beans	fresh, tender in julienne cut
1	onion	medium, thinly sliced
5 slices	ginger root	fresh, thin slices, finely julienned
5 strips	navel orange	thin strips of zest, julienned
3 cloves	garlic	minced
½ teaspoon	crushed chillie	
1 teaspoon	ground cumin	freshly roasted
1 teaspoon	whole cumin	
1 teaspoon	ground fennel seed	freshly roasted
¼ cup	orange juice, white wine or chicken stock	
1 teaspoon	salt	
1 teaspoon	pepper	
2 Tablespoons	Olive oil	
¼ cup	hot water or warm chicken broth	
1 Tablespoon	Maldive fish*	
1 pat	butter	

*available in Sri Lankan grocery shops

PREPARATION

- Heat Olive oil in sauté pan @ medium high. Keep this temperature throughout.
- Add whole cumin.
- After a few seconds, add onions & garlic, & stir.
- Add ground fennel seed; & stir.
- Now add cumin powder, crushed chillie, salt & pepper.
- Add beans, & stir well ensuring every piece is coated with the aromatic mix.
- Keep stirring for another few seconds until the green beans turn a nice dark green.
- Cover, & let cook for a minute or two.
- Uncover & stir the beans; add the Maldive fish; mix well.
- Add the hot water / chicken broth, & cover the pan immediately.
- Let cook for 2-3 minutes.

- Uncover & stir well; add ginger & orange zest; stir well; let the caramelized onions stick to the bottom of the pan.
- Now deglaze with orange juice or white wine.
- Stir the beans again, & finish cooking with a pat of butter
- Transfer the beans into a wide dish; leave uncovered

SERVING SUGGESTIONS

- On a bed of couscous
- as a side-dish for a rice 'n curry meal

Remember, even for those who are prone to gas attacks, this is quite a friendly recipe, because of the combination of ginger & fennel seeds.

Vegetable Curries

LEEKS WITH SHREDDED SWEET POTATOES

INGREDIENTS

1 bunch	leek greens	washed, dried & finely shredded
½	sweet potato	medium, peeled & shredded, using the box grater
2 cloves	garlic	finely sliced
1 Tablespoon	tiny dried shrimp	
1 teaspoon	fennel powder	
¼ teaspoon	crushed chillie	
1 Tablespoon	Olive oil	
¼ teaspoon	salt	
½ teaspoon	black pepper	freshly ground

PREPARATION

- Wash leek greens in a sink full of cold water. Drain well. Pat-dry, using paper towels or a kitchen towel.
- Stack in a neat bunch, & shred as finely as possible.
- Heat a non-stick sauté pan, & add the Olive oil . Add garlic, shrimp & crushed chillies.
- Add shredded leeks while stirring.
- Next add the shredded sweet potatoes, & stir well.
- Sprinkle salt, pepper & fennel powder, & continue to stir.
- Loosely cover the pan for a few seconds; uncover & continue to stir.
- If needed, sprinkle a Tablespoon of orange juice; stir well, & turn off the heat.

SERVING SUGGESTIONS

- A healthy side dish for a rice & curry meal, or with noodles or couscous.
- Can be used as a sandwich stuffing, a very healthy one at that!

MIXED VEGETABLE CURRY IN A HURRY!
With leftover roasted vegetable

INGREDIENTS

Any leftover roasted vegetable (e.g., tomatoes, eggplant) could be added to this curry.

½	long (i.e., Chinese) turnip	thinly sliced
½ bulb	anise (leftover)	thinly sliced
3 cloves	garlic	chopped
2 Tablespoons	Olive oil	
	salt & pepper to taste	
1 teaspoon	coriander powder	
1 teaspoon	cumin powder	
¼ teaspoon	turmeric	
2	green chillies	thinly sliced
2 slices	ginger	julienned
¼ cup	water	
⅓ cup	milk	

PREPARATION

- Heat Olive oil in a sauté pan @ medium-high; add sliced anise & garlic. Stir.
- Add sliced turnips, salt 'n pepper, curry powder & turmeric; stir well, & turn down the heat, add green chillies, ginger & the water. Stir well, & let cook, covered (for a few seconds).
- Add tomatoes & the eggplant, & mix well.
- Add the milk; stir, cover & let cook. Turn down heat to low.
- Check for flavour & doneness of turnip. Give a final stir, turn off the heat, & leave the pan covered.

SERVING SUGGESTIONS

- As a side dish for rice or pasta.
- Excellent vegetarian dish, with fresh bread or naan.

To make it a complete vegetarian meal, add a can of kidney beans (red or white), rinsed & drained.

Vegetable Curries

GREEN BEANS – WITH NO GAS!

THE STORY BEHIND

As I was growing up in Sri Lanka, we had curried fresh green beans a few times a week. With rice & curry, it's a nice side dish to go, with meat or fish. Of course, we bought the beans daily at the market or from the vegetable vendor who came to our door. Once you become a regular customer, the vendor would take pride in bringing you the freshest produce he could get.

Green beans can be cooked as a short curry or a long curry. A short curry has less gravy than the long curry. I personally like the short curry as it has more flavour & a nice creamy texture once it's cooked with a bit of coconut milk. But in recent years, I have found out, painfully, that this delicious vegetable causes gas in my stomach! So I came up with this recipe that took care of the nasty old gas.

INGREDIENTS

1 lb.	fresh green beans	washed & thinly sliced
2 Tablespoons	Olive oil	
1 teaspoon	sea salt	
1 teaspoon	black pepper	freshly ground
2 teaspoons	fennel seeds	freshly ground
1 teaspoon	crushed chillie	(optional)
1 sprig	curry leaves	
1 teaspoon	coriander	freshly ground
1 teaspoon	mustard powder	
1 Tablespoon	small dried shrimp	
3 cloves	garlic	minced
¼ cup	hot water or vegetable broth	
1 Tablespoon	plain yogurt	(no-fat or regular)
2 teaspoons	fresh ginger	minced

PREPARATION

- Wash, trim & clean the green beans. On a cutting board line them up a few at a time & cut as thin as possible.
- Heat oil in sauté pan at medium heat.
- Add garlic & curry leaves. Cook stirring.
- Add the beans & keep stirring.
- Add salt, pepper, chillie, coriander, fennel, minced ginger, dried shrimp & mustard powder. Keep stirring until all ingredients are well coated with oil.
- Add water or broth. Give it a good stir, cover & cook for about five minutes.
- Uncover, taste for seasoning, turn off the heat & fold in the yogurt. Keep uncovered until it comes to room temperature.

SERVING SUGGESTIONS

- Serve over couscous or steamed rice or with rice noodles.

Vegetable Curries

LASAGNA WITHOUT PASTA! WITH EGGPLANT, ZUCCHINI & SWEET RED PEPPER

"... a comfort food for my children"

INGREDIENTS

4 to 5	eggplants	small, dark purple, light purple or white, thinly sliced
1 teaspoon	salt	
1 teaspoon	black pepper	
1 Tablespoon	lemon or lime juice	
2	Zucchini	medium sliced length-wise
1	purple onion	thinly sliced
2	sweet red Sheppard-peppers or bell-peppers	cut in thin rounds
2	plum-tomatoes	ripe, thinly sliced
2 Tablespoons	Olive oil	
1 cup	light mozzarella cheese	grated
½ cup	light cheddar cheese	grated
½ cup	light smoked provolone cheese	grated
1 ½ cup	extra lean ground beef	cooked in stewed tomatoes, celery, green peppers & onions

All vegetables to be diced finely, and mildly flavoured with spices & herbs.

PREPARATION

- Put sliced eggplants in a medium bowl and sprinkle some salt & pepper, and a squirt of lemon juice. Set aside.
- Pour one tablespoon of Olive oil into the bottom of a med. size casserole dish & spread oil all over the casserole dish.
- Place a layer of sliced purple onions & then a layer of sliced eggplants.
- Spread a layer of mozzarella cheese on top of the eggplants.
- Sprinkle a dash of black pepper.
- Spread a layer of cooked ground beef.
- (for a vegetarian version: omit beef & add a mixture of beans, tofu & finely diced vegetables).
- Add a layer of sliced zucchini & add a dash of salt & pepper.
- Spread another layer of eggplants (if there's any left) or add another layer of ground meat mixture.
- Add another layer of onions, then another layer of red peppers, & then a layer of tomatoes.
- Spread the rest of the cheese on top if preferred add a dash of crushed chillies on top of tomatoes.
- Bake uncovered at 375 oven, for 45- 50 minutes.

GROUND BEEF FILLING
INGREDIENTS

2 lb.	extra lean ground beef	
1	large onion	diced
3 cloves	garlic	minced
½ teaspoon	salt	
½ teaspoon	black pepper	
1 teaspoon	freshly ground coriander	
1 teaspoon	freshly ground cumin	
1 teaspoon	red chillie pepper	
1 teaspoon	crushed chillies	
1 pinch	nutmeg	
1	medium zucchini	finely diced
1	medium carrot	finely diced
1	green pepper	finely diced
2 teaspoons	Olive oil	
1 7oz. can	tomato paste	
1 cup	diced tomatoes	fresh or canned
1 1" piece	cinnamon	
1 bay leaf		

PREPARATION

- Heat oil, in Dutch oven, at medium heat.
- Add ground beef & stir, breaking up the clumps of meat.
- Add salt & pepper, chillie powder, onions & garlic & the piece of cinnamon.
- Cook, stirring, until meat is dark brown Do not cover.
- Add coriander, cumin, nutmeg & bay leaf.
- Stir thoroughly.
- Cover, & let cook for about five minutes.
- Add zucchini & carrots. Stir well.
- When meat starts rendering juice, add tomato paste & the diced tomatoes.
- Mix well & add crushed chillies & continue to stir.
- Turn down heat, & continue to cook, covered.
- During the last five minutes, add the diced green peppers, & mix thoroughly.
- Cover & turn off the heat.

My children thoroughly enjoyed this dish, and it turned out to be one of their comfort foods.

Vegetable Curries

LENTIL CURRY
A perfect supper for 2.

Don't be discouraged by the long list of ingredients. This is a fast & easy recipe, and vegetarian if you kept out Panchetta.

INGREDIENTS

2 cups	lentils	picked*, washed**
1	carrot	diced
1	onion	medium, diced
2 cloves	garlic	sliced
2 teaspoons	mustard seeds	
2 teaspoons	sea salt to taste	
2 teaspoons	black pepper to taste	
¼ teaspoon	turmeric	
2	green chillies	fresh or frozen, sliced
2 teaspoons	Maldive fish chips***	
2 1" piece	cinnamon	
2 Tablespoons	Olive oil	
1 Tablespoon	panchetta	(optional) diced
1 cup	hot skim or 1% milk	
2 cups	hot water or chicken, (OR veggie broth)	
1 sprig	curry leaves	(available at Indian grocery shops)

* Pick lentils for stones & grit before soaking (see next).
** to cut down the 'gas' effect of lentils, soak for 12 to 30 mts. before cooking.
*** Available at Sri Lankan grocery stores.

PREPARATION

- In a medium saucepan, heat oil at medium high.
- Add the panchetta & cook stirring for 2 minutes.
- Add the mustard seeds.
- When they start popping, add the garlic & curry leaves.
- While stirring, add onions & the two pieces of cinnamon.
- Add the cleaned lentils & stir well until all ingredients are mixed.
- Turn down heat to medium.
- Add green chillies & carrots, & mix well.
- Cover & let cook for about 2 minutes.
- Uncover, stir & add the hot water or the broth.
- Let it cook, leaving the lid ajar (checking from time to time if the lentils are soft).
- Add Maldive fish & turmeric, & stir well.
- Cover & cook for another 3 minutes.
- Uncover, add hot milk & stir well.
- Check taste for seasoning, adding, if needed, a good squirt of lime juice.
- Take the saucepan off the burner.

VARIATIONS

a. If desired, a cup of warm coconut milk (canned or fresh) can be add instead of milk.

b. Instead of limejuice two Tablespoon of yogurt can be added as soon as the saucepan is
off the burner. Fold the yogurt gently into the lentil curry.

c. If desired as a final step one teaspoon of roasted curry powder can be sprinkled over
the hot lentil curry. (Refer to the recipe for the roasted curry powder).

A PERFECT SUPPER FOR TWO

We enjoyed this meal so much that I thought I'd write it down for you. I created this meal around the things I had in my fridge except for the 2 salmon steaks I just bought at the fish counter.

Vegetable Curries

SAUTÉED BROCCOLI, PERFUMED WITH AROMATIC NUTMEG

INGREDIENTS

1 bunch	broccoli	cut into florets; with green stems peeled & cut into matchsticks
3 to 4 slices	fresh ginger	julienned
2 cloves	garlic	thinly sliced
2 gratings	nutmeg	
2 teaspoons	Olive oil	
3 Tablespoons	warm water	
	salt & pepper	(Optional):

PREPARATION

- Wash broccoli, & let it drain.
- Heat a non-stick sauté pan.
- Add oil & garlic.
- When the garlic begins to sizzle, add broccoli & ginger.
- Stir well to coat all pieces in oil & condiments.
- Cover & cook for a minute at medium high.
- Uncover, stir & add the warm water. Cover <u>immediately</u>.
- Let cook for about 3 minutes . Uncover, & add the nutmeg. Stir well.
- Check for crisp tenderness. Turn off heat.
- Transfer broccoli onto a serving platter. DO NOT COVER (if you want to retain the eye-pleasing green of the broccoli).

To make it a complete stir-fry dish, add the following:

- A handful of carrot, sliced thin.
- A red pepper, cut into thin strips.

HEALTH BENEFIT

Ginger prevents gas! Nutmeg gives broccoli an appetizing aroma.

SERVING SUGGESTIONS

- Serve as a side dish with roasted meat or pan-fried fish as the main dish.

Vegetable Curries

SAUTÉED LEEK GREENS
Yummy & colourful!

INGREDIENTS

1 bunch	leek greens, washed in cold water
½ teaspoon	salt
½ teaspoon	pepper
½ teaspoon	crushed chillies
1 teaspoon	Maldive fish chips*
1 Tablespoon	Olive oil
2 cloves	garlic minced
1 dash	freshly grated nutmeg

* Available at Sri Lankan stores. If not, you can add really tiny dried shrimps, available at Chinese groceries.

PREPARATION

- Fill the kitchen sink with cold water, & wash the leek greens thoroughly. Drain well.
- In batches, bundle them up & cut into shreds. Thinner the better. The leeks cook faster retaining its dark green colour and valuable nutrients.
- Heat up a sauté pan at medium high heat. Add the Olive oil.
- Add minced garlic & crushed chillies.
- Add the shredded leek greens & stir well. Sprinkle salt & pepper.
- Keep stirring until the greens turn dark & get wilted. Sprinkle a dash of freshly grated nutmeg.
- Taste for doneness & transfer immediately to a serving dish.

SERVING SUGGESTIONS

- as a side dish for a rice & curry meal.
- on cooked pasta.
- on top of a whole wheat toast, tossed with shredded cheese.

STEAM STIR-FRIED SHREDDED CABBAGE & SWEET POTATO

INGREDIENTS

¼ of a	cabbage	small, washed & shredded
½ of a	sweet potato	medium, peeled & shredded
2½ teaspoons	fennel seeds	freshly ground
5 cloves	garlic	minced
5 thin slices	ginger	fresh, julienned
½ teaspoon	black or white	pepper
½ teaspoon	kosher salt	
2 Tablespoons	orange juice or apple cider	
1 Tablespoon	Maldive fish chips*	(optional)
1½ Tablespoons	Olive oil	

* available in Sri Lankan grocery stores

PREPARATION

- Heat Olive oil in a sauté pan at medium high.
- Add minced garlic & ginger.
- Stir cook for about 15 seconds.
- Add shredded cabbage & mix well with a pair of tongs. Tongs enable you to get hold of a whole bunch of cabbage & turn over. Keep stirring for about five minutes.
- Add salt, pepper, ground fennel & Maldive fish chips.
- Mix well. Splash 2 Tablespoon of orange juice or apple cider stir & let it cook covered for about 2 minutes.
- Now mix in the grated sweet potato & the rest of the Olive oil.
- Stir well.
- Turn down heat & let it cook, covered for about three to four minutes.
- Uncover.
- Add a dash of freshly grated nutmeg.
- If you like a little bite to it, add a pinch of cayenne pepper or even crushed chillies.
- Nutmeg adds a mouth watering aroma to the cooked cabbage
- Taste & check for seasoning.
- You might want to add a squirt of lemon juice for refreshing taste.

SERVING SUGGESTIONS

This preparation can be served as a side dish to
- a rice & curry meal;
- meat & potato meal;
- a meal of fish/ meat noodles; or
- an Italian-style sandwich.

Vegetable Curries

POTATOES FOR BRUNCH
Quick fix potato dish.

Serves three

Brunch is a popular meal for our family. For this meal, I always felt inspired to mix different kinds of vegetables in new blends of curry. I would somehow find a way to blend in the fruits as well – pineapple, apple, mango... Sometimes, five or six different new dishes got displayed on the brunch table. So they always looked forward to this feast.

INGREDIENTS

1	big baking potato (OR 2 red medium potatoes)	diced
½	purple onion	sliced
⅛	sweet red pepper	diced
1 teaspoon	crushed chillie	
½ teaspoon	chillie powder	
1 teaspoon	salt & pepper to taste	
2 cloves	garlic	sliced
1 1" piece	cinnamon	
2 Tablespoons	Olive oil	
1 handful	frozen green peas (optional)	
1 squirt	lemon juice	

PREPARATION

- Heat oil in a non-stick sauté pan & add the diced potatoes.
- Give it a good stir.
- Now add the diced garlic, salt, chillies, & pepper & cinnamon.
- Cover & cook for about 2 minutes .
- Uncover & stir well.
- Add onions & the peppers.
- Stir again. Reduce heat to medium.
- Cover & cook for another few minutes.
- Add, for colour contrast, a handful of frozen green peas.
- Stir well, cover, & cook for another 5 minutes.
- Uncover & check if the potatoes are cooked.
- Give it a squirt of lemon juice & serve as a side dish.

SERVING SUGGESTIONS

- This quick fix potato dish can be an accompaniment to eggs & bacon or just eggs & a crisp salad with whole wheat toast.

PUMPKIN CURRY
Sweet & spicy at the same time!

A PERSONAL ANECDOTE

In Sri Lanka, a pumpkin curry is the standard item served to close relatives invited home following a funeral. The potassium in the pumpkin presumably helps strengthen the heart muscle after a long and exhausting day of grieving. In addition to the pumpkin curry, the meal is made up of a very tasty serving of pol sambol (see Recipe in this book), dried fish curry and pickled vegetables. After this simply delicious meal following my mother-in-law's funeral, everyone was in a very calm mood.

INGREDIENTS

1 lb	pumpkin	
2	green chillies	seeded & diced
1 teaspoon	mustard	ground
1 teaspoon	cumin powder	
1 teaspoon	chillie powder	
2 teaspoons	coriander power	
2 1" pieces	cinnamon	
½ teaspoon	black pepper	coarsely ground
1 teaspoon	fenugreek	soaked in warm water
1 pinch	turmeric	
1	onion	medium, sliced
1 Tablespoon	Maldive fish	(optional)
3 cloves	garlic	sliced
½ teaspoon	white sugar	
½ cup	water	
1 cup	coconut milk	(powdered or canned but unsweetened)
¼ to ½ cup	coconut milk	(powdered or canned, but in thicker density)
1 teaspoon	salt	
1 teaspoon	spice blend	roasted aromatic

PREPARATION

- Soak the pumpkin in a big bowl of cold water, brush skin thoroughly (but NOT peel) pumpkin into 2" cubes.
- In a medium saucepan, assemble the pumpkin & all the spices (fenugreek, garlic, onion, salt, curry leaves, cumin, coriander, chillie powder, mustard powder, cinnamon, black pepper, sugar & Maldive fish); pour water & mix well.
- Cover & cook until the pumpkin is half-done. (Check with fork to see that it's not too mushy.)
- Uncover. Add coconut milk & green chillies, & give it a good stir. Cover, & cook for another 5 minutes .
- Add the rest of the milk, stir well, turn up heat, & let it come to a soft boil.
- Now, sprinkle roasted curry powder, cover, & turn off the heat.

SERVING SUGGESTIONS

- as a colourful & mouth-watering gravy dish, with rice & curry.

NOTE

When choosing pumpkin for this curry, pick one with green & yellow skin. Shh! Don't say I said it. They're more flavourful. So, in a curry, they taste sweet & spicy at the same time.

Vegetable Curries

SAUTÉED LONG BEANS (MAE-KARAL)
(In Onions & Dried Shrimp)

Exotic and flavourful. Trust me!

INGREDIENTS

1 lb (OR bunch)	long beans*	fresh
1 teaspoon	crushed chillies	
2 teaspoons	coriander powder	
2 teaspoons	cumin powder	
½ teaspoon	turmeric	
½ teaspoon	black mustard	freshly ground
¼ teaspoon	black pepper	freshly ground
1 teaspoon	fennel seed	freshly ground
1	onion	medium, sliced finely
2 Tablespoons	dried small shrimp	
1 sprig	curry leaves	
1 slice	ginger	chopped
3 cloves	garlic	minced
1 Tablespoon	Canola oil or Olive oil	
¼ cup	water or, chicken or vegetable broth	
½ teaspoon	salt	

* Available in Asian & regular supermarkets

PREPARATION

- Trim the two ends of the long beans, hold them in bundles & cut into 1" pieces.
- Wash well, & drain in a colander; set aside. Blot dry with a kitchen towel.
- Heat oil in a sauté pan at medium-high.
- Add onions, garlic, ginger, curry leaves & dried shrimp; stir & cook for a few seconds.
- Add beans & stir well; cover, & cook for 2 – 3 minutes.
- Uncover, & add cumin, coriander, mustard, turmeric, crushed chillies, ground fennel seed & salt 'n pepper; stir well.
- Add broth or water & cover.
- Turn the heat down a bit; let cook for about 7 minutes.
- Uncover, & taste for doneness & seasoning; turn off heat.

SERVING SUGGESTIONS

- As a side dish for noodles or rice.
- In a crusty Italian bun, replacing lettuce.

Fresh Mae-Karal

Cooked Mae-Karal

Vegetable Curries

SWEET 'N SOUR CABBAGE
Délicieux!

INGREDIENTS

¼	green cabbage	shredded
¼ teaspoon	fenugreek* powder	
1 teaspoon	cumin seed	
1 Tablespoon	vegetable oil	
1 teaspoon	vegetable oil	
4 cloves	garlic	sliced
1 teaspoon	black mustard seed	
¼ teaspoon	caraway seeds	
⅛ teaspoon	turmeric	
1 teaspoon	ground fennel	
2 teaspoons	ground coriander	
½ teaspoon	black pepper	freshly ground
1 teaspoon	sea-salt or kosher-salt	
1	medium purple onion	sliced
2 1" pieces	cinnamon	
2 Tablespoons	pancetta	shredded
	(OR lean ham)	
¼ cup	rice wine vinegar	
⅛ teaspoon	crushed chillies	(optional)
2 teaspoons	white sugar	
	juice of half a lemon	
1 Tablespoon	raisin	
1–1 ½ cup	warm water	

* Available in Indian grocery stores. Look for 'methi' – that's what they call it.

PREPARATION

- In a sauté pan, at medium heat, heat vegetable oil.
- Add mustard, cumin, garlic & fenugreek. Cook stirring.
- Add cabbage. Cook stirring.
- Add coriander, caraway, salt & pepper. Mix well.
- Add hot water, & put the lid on. Cook for 2 minutes, and then add cinnamon.
- Uncover & stir well. Add vinegar, give it a good stir, & put lid back on. Let cook for 2 minutes .
- Uncover, add raisins & sugar, & mix well. Let cook until cabbage is wilted.
- Empty the cabbage into a bowl.
- Add 1 teaspoon vegetable oil into the sauté pan. Add the pancetta or shredded cooked ham. Cook until crisp.
- Add the sliced purple onion. Sprinkle sugar over the onions. Let cook uncovered. When the onions are caramelized, add the cabbage back into the sauté pan, & mix well. Turn up the heat, & cook stirring, for a few seconds.
- Turn down the heat, & put the lid back on, & let cook for a few seconds.
- Uncover, & sprinkle lemon juice. Check for seasoning, & turn off the heat.

SERVING SUGGESTIONS

- On toasted Italian bread, with your choice of cold cut.
- As a side dish for a rice & curry meal.
- As a side dish for a meal with pork chops or roasted chicken.

SWEET POTATO & ZUCCHINI CURRY

INGREDIENTS

1	sweet potato	medium, peeled, & diced in 1" cubes
2	zucchini	medium, diced in 1" cubes
1	cooking onion	medium, diced
1 teaspoon	garlic	chopped
1 sprig	curry leaves	
1 teaspoon	kosher salt	
1 teaspoon	pepper	
½ teaspoon	crushed chillies	
2 teaspoons	coriander powder	
1 teaspoon	cumin powder	
1 teaspoon	curry powder	roasted
½ teaspoon	tumeric	
1 1" piece	cinnamon	
½ teaspoon	fenugreek*	
2 teaspoons	split mung-beans**	roasted
¼ cup	warm water	
1 cup	1% milk (OR powdered coconut milk)	
2 Tablespoons	Canola or Olive oil	

* Available in Indian grocery stores; ask for 'methi'.
** Also available in Indian grocery stores.

PREPARATION

- Heat oil in a saucepan @ medium high.
- Add onion, garlic, mung-beans, curry leaves, crushed chillies & fenugreek; stir well.
- Let cook, turning occasionally, for about a minute.
- Add cinnamon, diced sweet potatoes, & stir; cover & let cook for another 3 minutes.
- Add the ¼ cup warm water, stir well & cover. Give it another minute.
- Now, add the diced zucchini. (Do not mix. Leave them on top of the potatoes) Put the lid back on, & let cook for 1-2 minutes.
- Uncover; add coriander, cumin, roasted curry powder, turmeric, salt & pepper, & the dried shrimp.
- Put the lid back on. Let cook for a minute.
- Uncover, & add milk. Stir the vegetables well, & check for seasoning. If needed, add a bit more kosher salt.
- Let the sauce come to a gentle boil on low medium heat. Turn off the heat, & serve.

SERVING SUGGESTIONS

- As a side dish, with pasta, rice, naan or noodles.

NOTE

I serve this as a side dish with kiri-buth (milkrice) (see Recipe in this book), a must on New Year's Day. It goes well with the chicken curry & seeni sambol (i.e., spicy caramalized onion). (See Recipe in this book.)

Vegetable Curries

VEGETABLE STEW
For a feel good meatless meal!

INGREDIENTS

2	red or Yukon Gold potatoes	cubed
1	sweet potato	medium, cubed
2 stalks	celery	washed & diced
½ can	chick peas	washed & drained
1 cup	frozen mixed vegetables	
1 cup	frozen lima beans	
5 cloves	garlic	chopped
3	spring onions	chopped
2 Tablespoons	Olive oil	
2 teaspoons	cumin powder	freshly ground
2 teaspoons	coriander powder	freshly ground
2 teaspoons	black pepper	freshly ground
1 teaspoon	turmeric powder	
2 teaspoons	mustard powder	
2 teaspoons	crushed chillies	
1 teaspoon	salt	
2	bay leaves	fresh
	(OR 1 sprig curry leaves)	
1 cup	hot milk	(add more, if needed)
1 ½ cups	okra	

PREPARATION

- Heat Olive oil in a Dutch Oven or a deep sauté pan.
- Add onion, garlic & bay leaves (curry leaves). Cook stirring.
- Add the potatoes (both kinds). Stir, cover & cook for 4 to 5 minutes at medium high.
- Add lima beans, okra & mixed veggies. Stir, cover & let cook for about 3 minutes.
- Uncover, & add ¼ cup hot milk. Add cumin, coriander, turmeric & mustard & stir well. Cover & cook until the vegetables are soft & the broth is thickened.

SERVING SUGGESTIONS

- Warm crusty bread, pita or roti tastes divine with this stew. You'll feel good, too, for making another meatless meal for your family.

Vegetable Curries

String hoppers (in place of rice) & curries.

Rice & Noodles

I invite you to be fearless in experimenting with the many varieties of rice available to us from different parts of the world. There is no need to bore yourself with Uncle Ben's rice and Jasmine rice all the time!

First, there is red and black rice with all their natural goodness intact. Red rice, imported from Sri Lanka, comes in many varieties.

Then there are the many variations of Basmati rice from India and Pakistan.

There's also the North American variety of wild rice. Though really a grass seed and not a grain like others, it is still full of fibre and essential nutrients.

In terms of dishes, Basmati rice from India, raw Red rice from Sri Lanka and wild rice from Canada can be combined to create a highly nutritious and exotic platter that can be eaten with roasted or curried meats, fish or vegetables.

For our Sri Lankan festive kiributh (see Recipe), I use Sri Lankan raw red rice. Basmati rice is my preference for my fried rice preparation. I make a mixed rice platter using Basmati with wild rice, separately cooked.

Then you may combine 2 cups of Basmati with 2 cups of red rice in 5 cups of water, just enough to be cooked in a small rice cooker. (Measurement is with the cup that comes with the rice cooker.) It turns up a perfectly delicious and nutritious batch of steamed rice in under 20 minutes.

For flavour and aroma, you may throw into the pot a few cardamoms and a few pieces of fresh rumpé, at the beginning of the cooking process.

One last tip, if you're cooking a variety of polished rice, don't forget to enrich it by adding a can of beans rinsed and drained. (There are many varieties of low sodium, organic canned beans out there in supermarkets and health food stores.) They definitely add nutrition, colour and flavour to your rice.

An important point to remember is that rice does not need sodium-laden soup cubes, stock or salt to make it edible. It is meant to be steamed in plain water. Still it tastes deliciously good!

Now to a few Recipes.

CITRUS-FLAVOURED SWEET WILD RICE
Delicious, & full of goodness!

INGREDIENTS

2 cups	wild rice	soaked overnight in cold water
4 cups	cold water	
¼ cup	raisins	dark or sultana
½	lime	zested
½	lemon	zested
1	orange	medium, zested
3-4 thin slices	ginger	fresh, julienned

The following could be added if served as a salad:

1	carrot	finely diced
1 stalk	celery	finely diced
1	red bell pepper	roasted, finely diced
1 small can	pineapple bits	drained
½ cup	pine nuts	roasted
	(OR walnuts)	

PREPARATION

- Drain wild rice off the soaking water. Wash thoroughly once more.
- Add 4 cups of cold water into a deep pot.
- Add the wild rice. Turn up heat to high and let cook.
- When it comes to a boil, tilt the lid.
- Give a stir occasionally.
- When there's no more liquid left, cover the lid tight, turn off the heat and leave it to fluff up.

PREPARATION for the salad

- Saute the diced veggies and add to the cooked wild rice.
- Mix well, and sprinkle with the toasted nuts.
- Sprinkle crumpled goat cheese or Greek feta cheese.

SERVING SUGGESTIONS

This is an excellent brunch dish.

FRIED RICE WITH A TWIST!

INGREDIENTS

5 cups*	Basmati rice**	
¼ cup	dried shrimp	medium
7 cups	chicken stock***	
1 teaspoon	whole cumin	
2 teaspoons	coriander	roasted & coarsely ground
½ teaspoon	peppercorn	
1 Tablespoon	ghee or butter	
2 Tablespoons	Canola or Olive oil	
1/8 teaspoon	turmeric	
3 1" inch piece	cinnamon	
4 pods	cardamom	
4 cloves		
1	onion	big, diced
1 sprig	curry leaves	
1 packet	sweet frozen green peas	
4 pieces	rumpé****	

*   Using cup that comes with a rice cooker.
** Alternate: 3 cups Basmati & 2 cups Uncle Ben's Converted rice.
*** This is only an approximate amount).
****   Available in Sri Lankan or Asian grocery stores.

PREPARATION

- Wash rice, handling delicately, about 3 times; drain well & set aside.
- Heat a big saucepan at medium high. Add ghee / butter. When hot, add curry leaves, rumpé, onions & shrimp. Fry until golden brown.
- Add spices and the aromatics. Cook stirring, turn down heat to medium. Add drained rice. Stir well. Do not cover.
- Cook stirring until rice grains are light, & slightly coloured. The longer you stir-fry rice, the nuttier it'll taste.
- Add stock, & bring to boil. When broth settles down to the level of rice, put lid on & turn down heat; & seal the lid with a tea towel to ensure that no steam escapes from the pot. Let cook until rice is fluffy & fragrant.

- Uncover, add the packet of frozen green peas, & mix well. Keep covered until ready to serve.

ADDITIONAL FLAVOUR-ENHANCER

- Add grilled or sautéed shrimp.
- Cubed chicken breast, cooked in onion and yogurt sauce.
- Shredded roast pork with caramelized onions.
- Halved and sautéed button mushrooms.

Coconuts, a staple ingredient in Sri Lankan cooking.

KIRIBUTH
A festive rice!

This is a festive rice prepared by Sri Lankans on special days like New Year (April 14) and January 1, or at Weddings, Birthdays and Anniversaries, or at stage of life events like the first day of school of a daughter or son, or the coming of age of a daughter or the 'letter reading' day of a child when the newest member of the family is introduced to the world of knowledge by an elder. But it doesn't stop anyone from enjoying a meal of kiributh any day of the year or with the least excuse! So here, then, is the much loved and highly revered 'milk rice' (kiributh). I know you'll love it.

INGREDIENTS

6 cups*	raw red rice**
3 teaspoons	salt
3-4 pods	cardamom, crushed
2 1" inch piece	cinnamon
1	large coconut milk****
	(OR 2 cans of canned coconut milk)***

* Using the cup that comes with a rice cooker, which is just half the regular cup measurement.
** Alternate: Basmati or Jasmine rice
*** Available in Sri Lankan or Asian grocery stores.
**** See instructions for the procedure under 'Pol Sambol' in 'Sambols' section in this book.

PRE-PREPARATION

Soak rice for 1 or 2 hours just prior to cooking.

PREPARATION

- Wash the [soaked] rice about 3 times, drain well & pour into a deep saucepan.
- If using the freshly grated coconut, add the 2nd or 3rd extract of the coconut milk with the cardamoms and salt.
- Let cook at medium high heat with lid on.
- When the level of milk is the same as the rice, add the first extract of the coconut milk, stir well, turn down the heat to medium low. Let cook until the grains are well-done and the mixture is a thick mass. There should be NO pockets of unabsorbed milk in the pot.

Kiributh, fish, parsley salad, lunumiris & vegetable curry.

- Check for seasoning and for doneness. Does a rice grain held between your thumb and index finger get mashed easily?
- Keep the pot covered and warm until you're ready to serve on to the platter.

If using the canned coconut milk:

- Mix the first can with water and add to the rice.
- Let cook at medium high heat with lid on.
- When the level of milk is the same as the rice, add the 2nd can and mix well.

- Finish cooking with the lid on at medium heat.
- Check for seasoning and for doneness. Does a rice grain held between your thumb and index finger get mashed easily?
- Turn off the heat and keep warm with lid on.
- When you're ready to serve, transfer the milk rice into a big enough platter, smoothen the top with a spatula or a piece of warmed up banana leaf* .
- Cut in diamond shape, of same size.

* Available in many an Asian grocery store.

Rice & Noodles

NOTE

With whatever milk, the milk rice should be cooked into one thick mass, and it should have a milky taste.

SERVING SUGGESTIONS

- With a fish curry.
- With a chicken curry.
- With a shrimp curry.
- With curried eggplant.
- With seeni-sambol (Recipe in this book).

Sweet tooth?
If you're looking to end on a sweet note, try the kiributh with pol-paeni (see Recipe in this book) or bananas.

Kiributh & lunumiris

SPAGHETTI WITH AN ATTITUDE!
Healthy and delicious; you will not miss your meat sauce!

INGREDIENTS

275 gr.	spaghettini	whole wheat and flax seed
1 big pot	boiling water	(no need to add salt)
½	red bell pepper	thinly sliced
1 stalk	leeks (white part)	thinly sliced
1	carrot	medium, grated coarsely
2-3 cups	cremini mushrooms	sliced coarsely
1 Tablespoon	butter or ghee	
1 Tablespoon	Olive oil	
¼ cup	chicken stock	
2 grates	nutmeg	
3 cloves	garlic	sliced
2 teaspoons	all-purpose flour	
½ cup	2% or whole milk	
	salt & pepper to taste	
1 Tablespoon	crushed chillies	(adjust to suit your taste)
2 teaspoons	tomato paste	

PREPARATION

- Heat oil in a non-stick sauté pan at medium high heat.
- Add the crushed chillies and garlic. Stir, and add the sliced leeks and cook stirring for a few seconds.
- Add the red bell pepper and carrot, and salt and pepper. Keep stirring. Turn off the heat and set aside.

To make the mushroom sauce:

- Heat butter and oil in a sauté pan at medium high heat. Add garlic and stir.
- Add the sliced mushrooms and stir well to make sure that every piece is coated with oil.
- Sprinkle some salt and pepper. Stir well and let cook uncovered for a few seconds.
- Sprinkle the flour and give it a good stir.
- Add the chicken stock and cook stirring until the sauce comes to a smooth gravy.
- Add the milk.
- Add nutmeg. Turn off the heat and set aside.
- When the spaghettini is cooked and drained, add to the carrot, leeks and red bell pepper mixture. Mix well.
- When you're ready to serve, transfer the spaghettini into a nice platter and pour the mushroom sauce over it.

Rice & Noodles

RICE VERMICELLI WITH STIR-FRIED VEGGIES
Oodles of flavour, but takes no time at all!

INGREDIENTS

1 half-packet	rice sticks*	
1	sweet bell pepper	cut into thin strips
1	carrot	medium, in matchstick cut
1	zucchini	medium, in matchstick cut
1	onion	medium, sliced
1	Japanese eggplant	in matchstick cut
2 Tablespoons	lite soya sauce	
1 Tablespoon	chillie sauce	
½ teaspoon	kosher salt	
½ teaspoon	black pepper	freshly ground
1 teaspoon	curry powder	
2 cloves	garlic	minced
3 Tablespoons	Canola or Olive oil	
1 bundle	green onions	diagonally sliced

* Available in any Asian grocery store.

PREPARATION

- Fill a medium saucepan with water (3/4 full).
- Boil the water at medium high heat.
- Separate 2 bundles from the packet of rice sticks and add to the boiling water.
- Drain and spread the cooked rice sticks on a cookie sheet. Sprinkle the soya sauce. Cover loosely with foil.
- Heat a sauté pan at medium high heat and add 1 Tablespoon of Olive oil and minced garlic. After 3 seconds, add sweet bell pepper, carrot and zucchini. Cook stirring.
- Transfer to a plate.
- Into the same saucepan, add the other Tablespoon of oil and stir fry the cut eggplant. Keep stirring at medium low heat.
- After about 3 minutes, add the cooked carrots, zucchini and bell pepper.
- Add salt and pepper to taste.
- Transfer to a plate.
- Heat the third Tablespoon of Olive oil in the same sauté pan at medium high heat.

- Sauté the onions, add the curry powder, and mix well. Loosen the rice sticks using tongs, then add to the onion mixture and stir well.
- Add the chillie sauce. Keep stirring and mixing..
- Add the green onions and give it a good stir. Cover and turn off the heat. Let the rice sticks fluff up for a few seconds before serving on to a platter.

Rice Vermicelli

Rice & Noodles

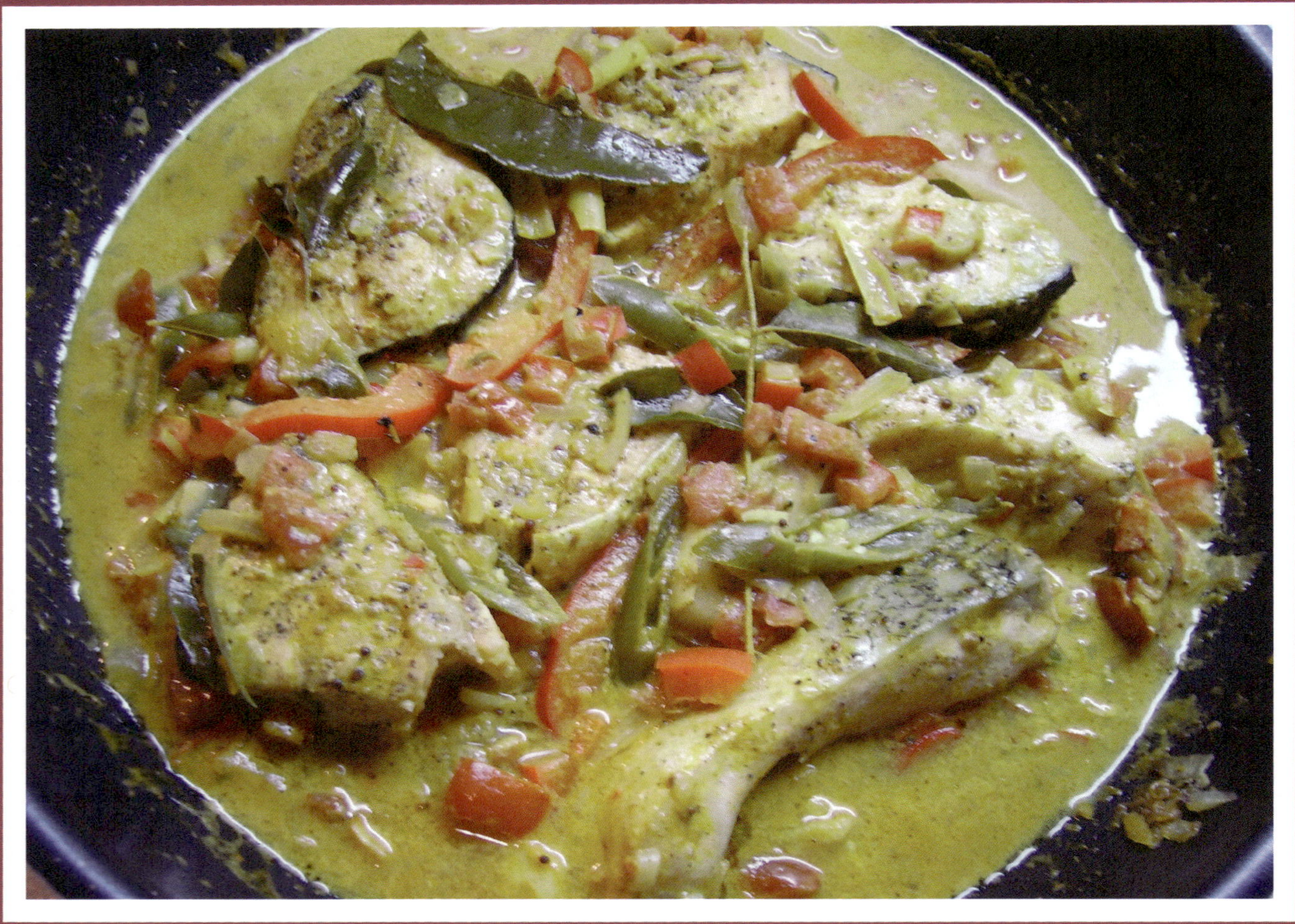

Fish Curries

BAKED SARDINE
FISH IN DARK TAMARIND SAUCE
KING FISH, HEAD & TAIL CURRIED
PAN-FRIED TILAPIA WITH ANISE-SCENTED CANNELLONI BEANS
PRAWN (SHRIMP) CURRY
SALMON CURRY IN A HURRY!
SPICY KING FISH CURRY
QUICK 'N EASY SHRIMP PREPARATION FOR TWO!

BAKED SARDINE

Flavour improves with time on this nostalgic favourite!

INGREDIENTS

1 lb	sardine	fresh or frozen, small or big
3 cloves	garlic	chopped
1	clove	
1	cardamom	
½ teaspoon	black pepper	freshly ground
3 teaspoons	chillie powder	
1 ½ teaspoons	sea salt	
2 Tablespoons	tamarind pulp*	
2 Tablespoons	Olive oil (OR vegetable oil)	
1	onion	medium, finely chopped
1 slice	ginger	finely chopped
¼ cup	warm water	

* Available at Asian grocery stores.

PREPARATION

- Clean & wash fish well.
- Dilute tamarind in warm water. Set aside.
- Grind all ingredients into a paste, except tamarind and oil.
- Mix with diluted tamarind.
- Coat fish well with the mixture.
- Pre-heat oven to 350 deg.
- Grease with oil a shallow baking pan, & place fish in it in one layer. Drizzle a squirt of Olive oil over the fish.
- Bake in the pre-heated oven for 15 to 20 minutes, or until the fish feels dry & done!

NOTE

Can be stored in the fridge for up to 2 weeks. As with any other meat or fish cooked in a sour-spicy sauce, flavour improves with time!

SERVING SUGGESTIONS

- With steamed rice, noodles, pasta or string hoppers.
- With warm, crusty bread or roti.

NOSTALGIC MEMORIES

This dish was the result of nostalgic memories growing up in Sri Lanka. We used to get fresh anchovies, or what we locally called sprats, in plenty, during the rainy season. Staying inside during the day in such wet and cold rainy weather made us feel ravenously hungry and we yearned for spicy warm snacks. This was one fish preparation that we drooled over with warm crusty bread (the bakery was just around the corner) or roti or even plain freshly grated coconut and steamed rice.

In this recipe, since I have failed to find a grit-free goraka, I've substituted tamarind sauce for the traditional 'goraka paste' (see Glossary).

Fish Curries

FISH IN DARK TAMARIND SAUCE

Yum yum! A healthy protein dish for a rice n' curry meal.

INGREDIENTS

1	whole pink salmon (OR tuna, or mackerel)	fresh or frozen
1	onion	medium, thinly sliced
2 2" pieces	cinnamon**	
3 cloves	garlic	chopped
2 Tablespoons	tamarind paste	
1 Tablespoon	curry powder	roasted
1 teaspoon	sea salt	
2 teaspoons	black pepper	freshly ground
2 teaspoons	chillie powder	
1 sprig	curry leaves	
2 pieces	rumpé*	
2 pieces	lemon grass*	
2 cups	warm water	

* Available in Sri Lankan or Asian grocery stores.
** Preferably Ceylon cinnamon. Its bark is soft, sweet and aromatic.

PREPARATION

- Slice the salmon, in its frozen form. Wash & drain.
- In a medium bowl, mix together salt, pepper curry powder, cinnamon, curry leaves, chillie powder, onion, garlic, rumpé & lemon grass; set aside.
- Mix tamarind paste with warm water, adding little at a time, until it turns into a velvety smooth paste. Next, thin it with more water. Now pour it into the curry mixture, & stir well with a spoon.
- Place the fish in a Dutch oven in single layer, & pour the curry mixture over the fish. Make sure every piece is coated well.
- Place the Dutch oven, at medium high heat. Cover, & let cook for about 5 to 7 minutes .
- Uncover, & turn each piece of fish, making sure they are well rolled in the dark gravy. Check for lunu ambul (salt & sour) taste. Add more salt & fresh lime juice to your taste. Turn down heat, & let simmer, covered for another few minutes . If you desire more gravy, this is the time to add more boiling water, making sure to mix it with the gravy. Cover, & turn off heat. If the gravy is cooked down, take the pan off the burner.

SERVING SUGGESTIONS

- With rice & curry, that includes
  o steamed Basmati rice
  o lentil curry
  o parsley sambol (Recipe in this book)
  o pappadum*
  o curried green beans &/or curried beetroot.

* See Glossary.

KING-FISH, HEAD & TAIL CURRIED
A fish curry at its best!

WITH BEACH-FRESH FISH ONLY

This is a very nostalgic dish. When we get a beach-fresh king-fish, my mother always made a separate curry of the fish head and the tail part. It was a fish curry at its best!

INGREDIENTS

1 head	of a large king-fish	cut into pieces
1 tail piece	of the same fish	cut into pieces
3 slices	fresh ginger	
2	green chillies	seeded & sliced
2	Kaffir-lime leaves	coarsely shredded
1 3" piece	lemon grass	bruised
2 teaspoons	chillie powder	
1 teaspoon	turmeric powder	
2 teaspoons	cumin powder	
1 teaspoon	coriander powder	
1 teaspoon	sweet cumin or fennel powder	
1	onion	medium, diced
1 sprig	curry leaves	
1 Teaspoon	lime juice	
1	tomato	diced
½ -1 cup	thick coconut milk	
1 cup	fish stock (OR thinly-constituted coconut milk)*	
1½ teaspoon	sea salt	
3 cloves	garlic	minced with ginger
1 teaspoon	fenugreek seed (OR powder)	
1 teaspoon	mustard powder	

* Use canned or powdered.

PREPARATION

- Cut up fish head into large pieces. (Much easier to have the fish-monger cut it for you.)
- Wash well using 1 teaspoon sea salt and lime juice.
- Place washed pieces of fish in a wide sauce pan or a Dutch oven, add all the condiments, aromatics and the flavour enhancers except the thick coconut milk.
- Put on stove at medium high heat, and cover. Let cook for 3 to 4 minutes.
- Uncover, and give the pot a good shake. And using a medium sized metal serving spoon, turn over the fish pieces. Cover and let cook for another few seconds.
- Uncover and add the thick coconut milk, and mix ingredients gently. Let the sauce come to a boil, turn off the heat.

SERVING SUGGESTIONS

- With steamed rice.
- With warm crusty bread, naan, or any variety (West Indian, East Indian or Sri Lankan) of roti.

PAN-FRIED TILAPIA WITH ANISE-SCENTED CANNELLONI BEANS

INGREDIENTS

4 pieces	Tilapia	cleaned & washed, & sprinkled with
	salt & pepper	to taste
1 bulb	anise	thinly sliced
2	purple onions	medium, thinly sliced
¼ cup	all-purpose flour	for dredging
¼ cup	coriander leaves	rough-chopped
1 teaspoon	fennel powder	
3 cloves	garlic	minced
2 slices	ginger	minced
1 pinch	crushed chillies	
½	lemon	juiced
4 Tablespoons	Olive oil	
2 Tablespoons	Olive oil	
1 14 oz can	white beans	rinsed & drained

PREPARATION

- Dry fish with paper towels. & sprinkle salt, pepper & fennel powder, on both sides.
- Lightly dredge in flour, & shake off excess flour from the fish.
- Heat a non-stick sauté pan to medium-high,. When hot, add 2 Tablespoons oil.
- Place fish in pan without crowding it. Let cook for 5 minutes . NO turning at this time.
- When both sides are golden brown, transfer into an oven-proof platter, & leave in oven at keep-warm temperature.
- Heat oil in sauté pan. Add anise, & stir well. Add onions, & salt & pepper to taste. Stir well.

- Add crushed chillies, garlic & ginger, & cook stirring. Cover & let cook until onions get caramelized. Add the beans & coriander leaves, Stir well, on low heat, for about 2 minutes, for the flavours to blend.
- Serve on to a platter, & place the warm fish on top, with wedges of lime or lemon.

SERVING SUGGESTIONS

- With salad greens.
- With a side dish of rice pilau.

Pan-fried Tilapia on a bed of Romaine lettuce.

PRAWN (SHRIMP) CURRY

PRE-PREPARATION of spice ingredients for an added fresh flavour.

This takes only a few minutes of your time. Gather the whole spices, put into your favourite spice grinder, and give it a good whirl.

- **Roast** all ingredients, except prawns, in a sauté pan, at low medium heat until golden brown.
- **Grind** the roasted ingredients, & mix well with the prepared prawns.
- **Sprinkle** 1 teaspoon salt, & a squirt of lemon juice.
- Set aside.

INGREDIENTS for Roasted Condiments

2	dry chillies (optional)
1 teaspoon	fenugreek
1 1" piece	cinnamon
1 1" piece	rumpé*
1 Tablespoon	coriander seeds
1 teaspoon	cumin seeds
1	clove
1	cardamom
1	dry curry leaves

* Available in Sri Lankan or Asian grocery stores.

INGREDIENTS

1 lb	large prawns	washed, shelled & de-veined
1	onion	chopped
2 thin slices	ginger	
3 cloves	garlic	sliced
2	green chillies	chopped
1 Tablespoon	Canola oil	
2 teaspoons	salt	
1 teaspoon	black pepper	freshly ground
2	Kafir lime leaves	bruised
8 ozs	coconut milk	(canned or powdered)
4 ozs	2% milk	
	juice of 1 lime	
2 pieces	goraka* (gambodge) (optional)	soaked & washed in warm water
	(OR 1 medium Roma tomato,	cut into wedges)

* See Glossary

PREPARATION

- Set burner to medium.
- Place saucepan, & add oil.
- add curry leaves & garlic first.
- Now add the rest of the ingredients, except coconut milk (& prawns).
- Sauté for 2 to 3 minutes.
- Add prawns; cook stirring for 2 minutes.
- Add both coconut milk, & 2%; cook stirring until it comes to a soft boil.
- Taste for seasoning. Add lime juice, & take pan off the heat.

SERVING SUGGESTIONS

- With rice & curry meal.
- With vermicelli and stir fried veggies.

QUICK 'N EASY SHRIMP PREPARATION FOR TWO!
Delicious!

INGREDIENTS

8	jumbo shrimps	easy-peel
1 teaspoon	lemon juice	
½ teaspoon	lemon rind	
1 teaspoon	black pepper	freshly ground
¼ teaspoon	grated ginger	
2 slices	ginger	
¼ teaspoon	sea salt or kosher salt	
1½	teaspoons	Canola oil
2 cloves	garlic	sliced
1	onion	medium, sliced
1 teaspoon	roasted coriander powder	
1 teaspoon	roasted cumin powder	
1 teaspoon	mustard powder	
¼ cup	red or white wine	
1 Tablespoon	oyster sauce	

PREPARATION

- Sprinkle shrimp with 1 teaspoon sea salt, add cold water, & wash & drain the shrimp well.
- Give a squirt of lemon juice.
- Add lemon rind, black pepper, ginger & salt. Give a stir, & set aside.
- In a sauté pan, heat oil at medium high. Add onion, garlic & ginger. Cook stirring for a few seconds. Add cumin, coriander & mustard powder. Stir well. Add shrimp, & stir well. Cook for about a minute . Add oyster sauce with the condiments & mix well.
- Turn the shrimp over & mix well, with the condiments, & turn down heat to low medium. Cover, & let cook for about 2 minutes . Turn off the heat. Transfer the warm aromatic shrimp into a nice platter. Bring on to the table.

SERVING SUGGESTIONS

- With steamed Basmati   rice or noodles.

Swarna wading through the tropical waters of Sri Lanka

Fish Curries

SALMON CURRY IN A HURRY!
An exotic flavour for a nice change - from grilled, baked or poached salmon.

INGREDIENTS

4	salmon steaks	
1 Tablespoon	Olive oil	
1	vine tomato	medium, diced
	(OR 2 roma tomatoes)	
1	onion	medium, sliced
2 cloves	garlic	minced
2 Tablespoons	lemon juice	(OR 1 Tablespoon lime juice)
	Salt & pepper to taste	
1 piece	cinnamon	
1 teaspoon	cumin	
1 teaspoon	coriander	
1 teaspoon	chillie powder	
½ teaspoon	turmeric	
2 leaves	Kaffir lime	
	(OR 1 sprig curry leaves, or zest of half a lemon)	

PREPARATION

- Wash salmon steaks in cold water, cut in half and dry with a paper towel. Sprinkle with salt & pepper.
- Mix cumin, coriander, chillie powder and turmeric.
- Rub the salmon steaks with the spice mixture. Set side.
- Heat oil in a saucepan and add the garlic and onion. Cook stirring.
- Now add the diced tomato and the green chillies and stir well. Cover and let cook at low medium heat for a minute or two.
- Uncover and add the fish pieces. Coat well with the condiments.
- If you have coconut milk powder on hand, mix about 3 Tablespoons with hot water and add to the fish. Stir ingredients gently so as not to break up the fish.
- Place the lid ajar and cook for a minute or two.
- Uncover and add the lime juice. Stir gently.
- Check for seasoning. Turn off the heat and transfer into a serving dish.

SERVING SUGGESTIONS

- With brown Basmati and wild rice.
- With converted Basmati rice
- With rice & beans.

NOTE

Brown Basmati and wild rice could be cooked mixed together. Just double the amount of water you use to cook ordinary rice. And keep the heat at medium low until the rice becomes tender.

Cooked rice could be easily frozen in a freezer bag for future use.

SPICY KING FISH CURRY
Try this for a tasty, all-rounded meal with steamed rice!

INGREDIENTS

4 steaks	King Fish (substitutes: cod, halibut, tuna or salmon)	
2 teaspoons	sea salt	
2 teaspoons	freshly ground black pepper	
2 teaspoons	chillie powder	
1 teaspoon	fennel powder	
1 teaspoon	roasted aromatic spice blend*	
2 teaspoons	tamarind paste	diluted
1 teaspoon	fenugreek seeds	
1 ½ teaspoons	Canola oil	
1 cup	warm water	
2 Tablespoons	lime juice	
1 Tablespoon	tomato paste	
1 1" chunk	ginger	minced
1 sprig	curry leaves	shredded
4 cloves	garlic	minced
1 2" piece	lemon grass	bruised

* See Recipe in this book.

PREPARATION

- Wash steaks in cold water about twice. Drain. Cut each steak in four. Squeeze half a lime over the fish. Mix well. Set aside, for about 5 minutes .
- Wash fish in cold water, & drain well. Set aside.
- Dilute tamarind in warm water. Mix with the spices.
- Pour oil in a wide sauté pan, & turn up the heat. Place fish in one layer in pan. Pour spice-tamarind mixture over the fish, making sure each piece is well-coated with the sauce.
- Cover, & let cook @ high medium for 2 minutes . Turn down heat to low medium.

- Uncover, add tomato paste, & stir into the sauce. Using a serving spoon, pour sauce over all the fish, & then turn each piece over.
- Cover & let cook again for another 10 minutes .
- Taste for seasoning. Turn off heat, leaving pot on burner until you're ready to serve.

SERVING SUGGESTIONS

A menu for a tasty, all-rounded meal, with
- steamed rice
- lentil curry
- parsley salad or kale mallung (see Recipes).

Spicy King Fish Curry

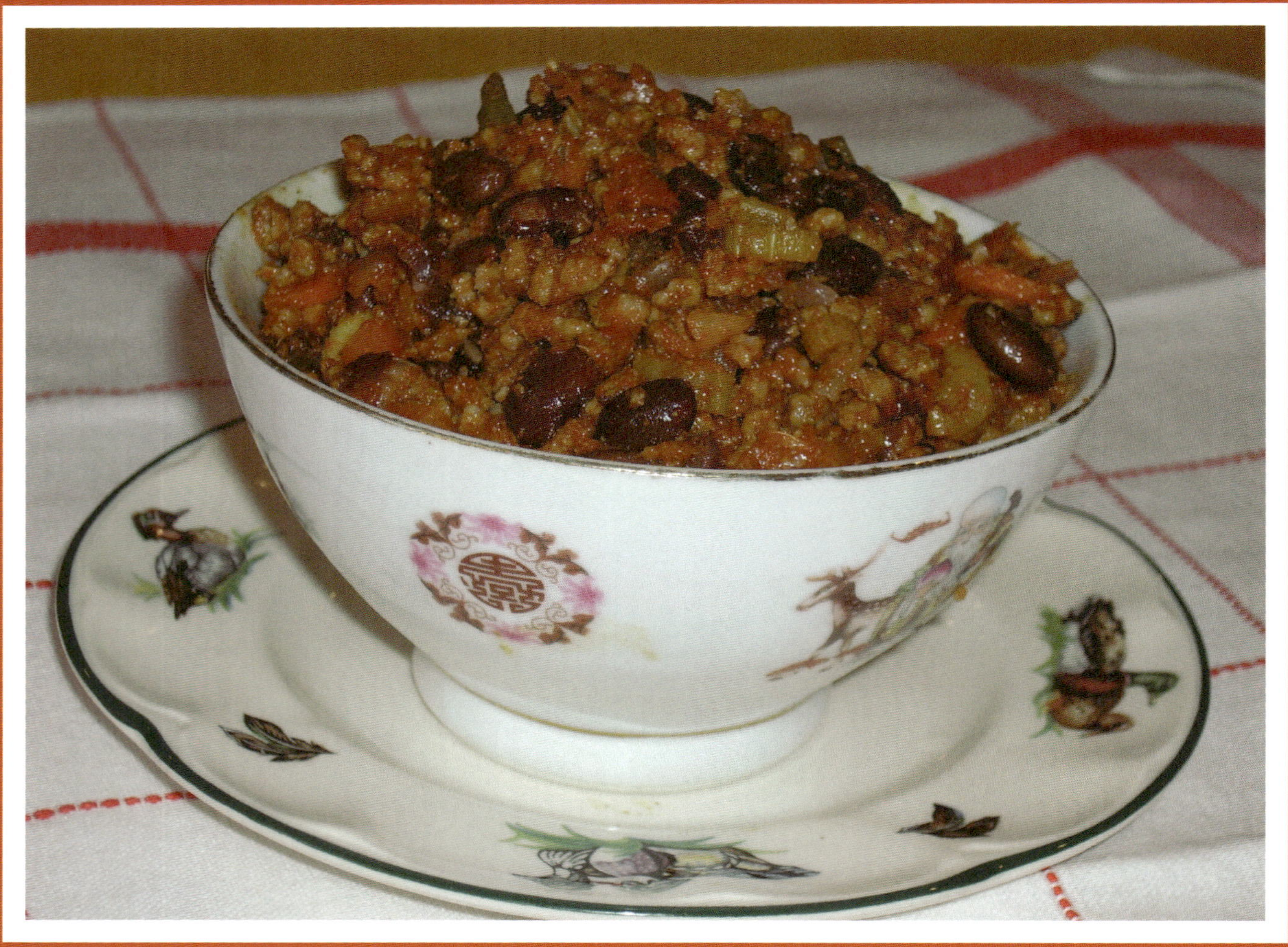

Meat Curries

BEEF CURRY IN A HURRY!
BEEF CURRY IN ZUCCHINI, ONIONS & TOMATO SAUCE
CALF LIVER WITH SAUTÉED ONIONS
GRANDMA'S FAMOUS BEEFSTEAK
GROUND SIRLOIN CURRY IN A HURRY
EGG WHITE CURRY
HAMBURGERS WITH A TWIST
MA'S GOURMET-FLAVOURED HEALTHY HAMBURGERS
MA'S WORLD-FAMOUS CHICKEN CURRY!
VEAL LIVER CURRY

BEEF CURRY IN A HURRY!

INGREDIENTS

1 package	beef	sliced for stir frying
	(OR beef slices cut	into thin strips)
1 teaspoon	salt	
1 teaspoon	pepper	freshly ground
1 teaspoon	tamarind preserve	(comes in a jar)*
2 teaspoons	curry powder	roasted (Recipe in this book.)
1	onion	medium, sliced
3 cloves	garlic	chopped
1	green chillie	diced
	(substitute: jalapeno pepper)	
2 2" pieces	cinnamon	
1 sprig	curry leaves	
	(OR 1 bay leaf)	
½ teaspoon	fenugreek	
	(OR fenugreek powder)**	
1 Tablespoon	Olive oil	
1 teaspoon	crushed chillies	
½ cup	hot water	
2 cups	beef or vegetable broth	
2	tomatoes	medium, diced
½	sweet bell pepper	(optional)
½	green bell pepper	(optional)
¼ cup	snow peas	(optional)

* Can be bought at any Indian or Sri Lankan grocery store. Has infinite shelf life!
** Available at Indian grocery stores.

PREPARATION

- Dilute tamarind preserve in hot water. Pour over the beef.
- Add salt, pepper and roasted curry powder. Mix well. Set aside.
- Heat oil in a saucepan, add curry leaves, fenugreek, chopped garlic, crushed chillies and onions.
- Sauté until translucent. Add green chillies and cinnamon.
- Stir well, turn down heat and let cook for another 5 minutes.
- Add beef and turn up the heat, and cook stirring.
- Add the beef broth, and cook covered for another few minutes.
- Uncover and add the diced tomatoes. Mix well and cover. Let cook at high medium 3 to 4 minutes.
- At this point, you can add strips of sweet bell pepper, green bell pepper and snow peas if desired.
- Cook for 2 minutes. Taste for seasoning. Remove pan from the heat and let it continue cooking in the heated saucepan.

SERVING SUGGESTIONS

- With fried rice, steamed rice, couscous or rice noodles.

Meat Curries

BEEF CURRY IN ZUCCHINI, ONIONS & TOMATO SAUCE
using sirloin grilling steak from the freezer

For the tomato sauce
INGREDIENTS

1 28 oz. can	Pastene tomatoes	
1	onion	medium, sliced
3-4 cloves	garlic	chopped
1 handful	flatleaf parsley	minced
1	carrot	large, grated coarsely
1 teaspoon	crushed chillies	
1 teaspoon	garam masala (home made)*	
2 Tablespoons	tomato paste	
1	bay leaf	
1 pinch	salt	
1 teaspoon	sugar	
1 teaspoon	pepper	freshly ground

* See Glossary

PREPARATION

- Sauté onion and garlic in a Tablespoon of Olive oil.
- Add crushed chillies and the garam masala.
- Add the tomato paste and mix well. Stir everything and let cook for 1-2 minutes.
- Add the canned tomatoes and bay leaf.
- Add sugar, salt and pepper and stir well.
- Add the grated carrot and stir cook. (If you have a smoked chorizo sausage, this is the time to add it, diced.)
- Turn down the heat and let cook for about 45 minutes.
- Add the chopped parsley, cover and let simmer.

For beef
PRE-PREPARATION

Cut the 2 steaks at a heavy angle. Put in a glass bowl and season with salt, pepper and soy sauce.

INGREDIENTS

2	sirloin grilling steaks	sliced at a heavy angle
½ teaspoon	salt	
½ teaspoon	pepper	
1 Tablespoon	soy sauce	
1 Tablespoon	Worchestershire sauce	
1	onion, red or white	large, sliced
1	zucchini	medium, cut in half, split, then cut into thin strips
1	carrot	small, grated coarsely
3 cloves	garlic	diced
1 ½ Tablespoons	Olive oil	(OR light Canola oil)
1 squirt	fish sauce	

PREPARATION

- In a non-stick sauté pan, heat oil at medium high.
- Add garlic, stir and add the seasoned meat. Place each slice of meat flat in the pan.
- Brown one side, then turn over.
- Sprinkle the Worchestershire sauce. Let it cook.
- Add the grated carrot. Cover and let cook for about 30 sec.
- Add the sliced onions. Add salt and pepper, and let cook for about a minute.
- Add some tomato sauce. Mix well.
- Place some zucchini strips on top and cover. Let cook for about a minute.
- Add another spoon of tomato sauce and another layer of zucchini strips on top. Smother the zucchini strips with the sauce.
- Turn down the heat, cover and cook for another 5-10 minutes. Turn off the heat.

SERVING SUGGESTIONS

- Serve on a bed of Basmati rice or steamed rice sticks, flavoured with a sprinkling of light soy sauce, fish sauce and olive oil.

Delicious!!!

Meat Curries

CALF LIVER WITH SAUTÉED ONIONS

INGREDIENTS

1 package	calf liver	washed & drained
	(5-7 thin liver steaks in package)	
¾ cup	milk	
1 cup	flour	for dredging
1 teaspoon	kosher salt or sea-salt	
2 teaspoons	black pepper	freshly ground
1 teaspoon	ginger	powdered
2 teaspoons	garlic powder	
1 teaspoon	chillie powder	
1 teaspoon	paprika	
¼ cup	Canola oil	

INGREDIENTS for sautéed onions

2	Vidalia onions	medium, sliced
½ teaspoon	salt	
½ teaspoon	pepper	
1 teaspoon	crushed chillies	
1 1" piece	cinnamon	
1 sprig	curry leaves	
1 teaspoon	rice vinegar	
2-3 cloves	garlic	minced

PREPARATION
For Liver Steak

- Add milk into a small glass dish, & immerse the liver, & leave in fridge for 20 minutes or more.
- In a bowl, combine all five ingredients, sprinkle over the drained & dried liver steak, & mix well. Set aside. Or leave it in the fridge for one hour.
- Spread flour on a plate, & dredge each liver steak lightly in flour.
- Fry in a shallow sauté pan, giving about 2 minutes per side. & drain on paper towel.

For Onions

- Heat oil in sauté pan.
- Add curry leaves, onion, garlic & cinnamon. Stir well. Add crush chillies, salt & pepper to taste. Cook stirring for about 5 minutes .
- Turn down the heat, & let onions caramalize.

SERVING SUGGESTIONS

- With mashed potatoes & steamed vegetables.

HEALTH BENEFIT

An excellent source of iron.

GRANDMA'S FAMOUS BEEFSTEAK
An aromatic & very flavourful meat dish!

INGREDIENTS

2 lbs	rump roast or sirloin steak	
2	onions	big, sliced thick
2	jalapeno peppers (OR green chillies)	seeded & sliced lengthwise
2 teaspoons	sea salt	
2 teaspoons	pepper	coarsely ground
2 teaspoons	coriander powder	freshly ground
2 teaspoons	cumin powder	
½ teaspoon	turmeric	
1 teaspoon	fenugreek powder	
1 teaspoon	fennel	freshly ground
2 teaspoons	chillie powder	
4 pods	cardamom	
1 sprig	curry leaves	
4 1" pieces	cinnamon	
3 1" pieces	lemongrass	bruised
¼ cup	red wine vinegar	
2 cups	cold water or beef broth	

NOTE

* Wash meat before cutting, & dry with paper towel. Put the meat in the freezer for about 20 minutes. This will make it easier to slice it thin.
* My mom used to pound the meat on the grinding stone. Then, adding salt & pepper, it would get a second pounding.

PREPARATION

- Slice meat against grain into thin 2" x 2" slices, even.
- Place the slices in a wide sauce pan, preferably in one layer. Add all ingredients, except sliced onions. Put the lid on, & turn the heat to high. Let the meat come to a simmer.
- Turn down the heat to medium. Uncover, & give it a good stir, & put the lid back on.
- Let cook for another 10 to 15 minutes , or until meat is soft. Check for seasoning. If more sour flavour is preferred, add 2 more Tablespoons of vinegar. If softer texture is desired, add a little more broth or warm water.
- Add half of the onions, cover & cook for another 5 minutes .
- Transfer meat into a platter.
- Put sauce pan back on the burner, at low medium heat, & add 1 Tablespoon of Canola oil.
- When it begins to sizzle, add the sprig of curry leaves, & the rest of the onions, & if a spicier flavour is desired, add a teaspoon of crushed chillies. Cook stirring for a few seconds, & mix the meat with sautéing onions. Cook stirring, check for seasoning, turn down the heat, & put the lid back on until ready to serve.

SERVING SUGGESTIONS

- As a side dish with rice.
- On a crusty bun, with a chopped salad.
- As a main dish with potatoes & green salad.

Meat Curries

GROUND SIRLOIN CURRY IN A HURRY!

INGREDIENTS

1–2 lbs	ground sirloin	
1	cooking onion	big, diced
½	green pepper	diced
½	zucchini	small, diced
1 small package	frozen corn	(if you happen to have it)
2 cups	diced canned tomatoes	
½ cup	diced fresh pineapple (could be substituted with canned pineapple bits)	
4 cloves	garlic	diced
1 teaspoon	sea salt	
1 teaspoon	black pepper	freshly ground
1 teaspoon	crushed chillies	
1–2 teaspoons	chillie powder	
1 ½ teaspoons	curry powder	roasted
2 1" pieces	cinnamon	
2 teaspoons	Canola oil	
2 Tablespoons	Sherry vinegar or Red wine vinegar	
1 Tablespoon	tomato paste	
2 Tablespoons	water	

PREPARATION

- Heat a sauté pan at medium high. Add the garlic & crushed chillies, & then the onion. Cook stirring.
- Add the beef into the mixture, breaking up the clumps; sprinkle the vinegar.
- Cover, & let cook 2 to 3 minutes, until meat is crusty brown.
- In the meantime, get the vegetables washed & diced.
- Uncover, & add the cinnamon. If needed, use a folk to break up the ground sirloin. Mix & add the spices, salt & pepper. Cover, & let cook until the meat is cooked.
- Uncover, & add the diced vegetables. Mix well. Add the diced tomatoes, along with the liquids. Let cook for about 2 minutes . Clear the center of the pan, add the tomato paste, & mix well. Cook stirring. Add chunks of pineapple. Cover, & let cook at simmer for about 3 minutes .
- Uncover, stir the meat well, & sprinkle the curry powder. Turn off the heat.

SERVING SUGGESTIONS

- On a bed of steamed Basmati rice.
- On cooked short pasta, like rigotoni.
- On a bun, with a layer of grated cheese.

HEALTH BENEFIT

For added nutrition, you can add a rinsed & drained can of beans (red, white or black) at the final stage of cooking. It's delicious, too!

Meat Curries

EGG WHITE CURRY

INGREDIENTS

8	eggs	hard-boiled, shelled
4 teaspoons	fenugreek	soaked in water
1 teaspoon	whole peppercorn	
1 teaspoon	sea salt	
1 teaspoon	ground rice	
¼ teaspoon	turmeric powder	(to desired colour)
1 Tablespoon	Maldive fish chips	
1	onion	medium, diced
1 sprig	curry leaves	coarsely chopped
1 piece	goraka*	washed thoroughly in warm water until grit-free
2 1" pieces	cinnamon	
2	green chillies	seeded & diced
2 pods	cardamom	slightly bruised
12 oz	coconut milk	thinner consistency (fresh, canned or powdered)
½ cup	coconut milk	thicker consistency (fresh, canned or powdered)
½ cup	whole milk or 2%	
1 grate	nutmeg	

* See Glossary. Available in Sri Lankan grocery stores. A good substitute might be 2 – 3 unpitted dried prunes (available in any grocery store).

PREPARATION

- In a medium sauce pan, on low-medium heat, cook uncovered in the thinner coconut milk, all ingredients except lime juice, eggs & the thicker milk. Keep stirring. Mix well to bring out the thickening effect of fenugreek. Add salt.
- Add the other milk, & cook stirring.
- Add the boiled eggs, bring to boil, add lime juice, taste for seasoning & take off the heat.

SERVING SUGGESTIONS

- With rice, as a protein plus gravy dish.
- With string hoppers (if you can find a Sri Lankan catering outlet).
- With steamed rice sticks (available in Asian grocery stores, and very inexpensive).

HAMBURGERS WITH A TWIST

INGREDIENTS

1 ½ lb	ground sirloin	
1 stalk	celery	chopped fine
½	granny smith apple	grated into the celery
1	onion	medium, grated onto the above mix
1 teaspoon	black pepper	freshly ground
1 teaspoon	sea salt or kosher salt	
1 Tablespoon	Worcestershire sauce	
3 cloves	garlic	finely chopped
1 Tablespoon	lemon	
1 Tablespoon	orange rind	
2 Tablespoons	tomato ketchup	
1 Tablespoon	Dijon mustard	
½ teaspoon	crushed chillies	(optional)
1 handful	bread crumbs	
1 handful	parsley	finely chopped
¼	sweet bell pepper	finely diced

PREPARATION

- In a medium bowl, mix all ingredients together. Set aside 10-20 minutes.
- Now, make hamburger patties.
- Heat a non-stick pan, at medium high, & give a squirt of Canola oil.
- Sizzle the patties 2 minutes per side. Test for doneness before turning off the heat.

SERVING SUGGESTIONS

- With home-made oven fries.
- On a crusty bun with a chopped salad.

Meat Curries

MA'S GOURMET-FLAVOURED HEALTHY HAMBURGERS
with healthy Home Fries, Mmm!!

HAMBURGERS: INGREDIENTS

1½ lbs	extra-lean ground beef	
¼	purple onion	finely chopped
¼ teaspoon	salt	
¼ teaspoon	black pepper	freshly ground
¼ teaspoon	chillie powder	
¼ teaspoon	sweet paprika powder	
1 teaspoon	Dijon mustard	
1	spring onion	chopped fine
2 cloves	garlic	chopped fine
1 Tablespoon	small shrimp	dried, finely chopped
1 Tablespoon	home-made bread crumbs	

PREPARATION

- Assemble all ingredients in a bowl, & mix well. Set aside.
- Divide the mixture into handfuls. Press into a patty on your palms. Set aside on a plate.
- Turn on the grill or grill pan. Rub, or spray, oil on the pan. When the pan begins to smoke, place the patties, one by one, without crowding. Cook until the patty is done.

FRIES: INGREDIENTS

2	Russet potatoes	big, peeled, washed & cut into lengthwise wedges. Immerse in coldwater as they are cut.
¼ teaspoon	garlic powder	
¼ teaspoon	chillie powder	
¼ teaspoon	sweet paprika powder	
¼ teaspoon	Italian herb seasoning	
pinch	coriander	ground
pinch	ground cumin	
pinch	ground fennel	

PREPARATION

- Pre-heat over to 400.
- Mix condiments in a small bowl.
- Cover a baking pan with a sheet of parchment.
- Place the potatoes in one layer. Sprinkle 1 ½ Tablespoon Olive oil on the potatoes. Sprinkle the spice mixture over it. Mix well. Re-arrange the potato wedges, still in one layer. Place in the pre-heated oven. Bake until the potatoes are golden brown (25 to 30 minutes).

DRESSING
for both hamburgers & fries

Mix together:

1 teaspoon	Dijon mustard
1 teaspoon	ketchup
1 teaspoon	mayonnaise (Hellman's)
1 Tablespoon	fat free yogurt
1 Tablespoon	freshly squeezed lemon juice
	salt & pepper to taste
1 Tablespoon	chopped green onions
1 pinch	fennel powder
1 pinch	cumin powder

SERVING SUGGESTIONS

- On crusty Italian buns, cut in half, fleshed out at the centre to get room for your patties & other condiments (sliced purple onions, shaves of fresh parmesan cheese, slices of granny smith apple & slices of vine-ripe tomatoes).

- With a salad –

½ bulb	fresh anise	grated
¼	purple onion	thinly sliced
3"	chunk English cucumber	
¼ cup	shredded Italian radicchio	
1 pinch	salt & pepper each	
1 Tablespoon	freshly squeezed lemon juice	

Give a scant sprinkle of Olive oil, & toss together. Voila!

Meat Curries

MA'S WORLD-FAMOUS CHICKEN CURRY!
an exotic Sri Lankan meal, without ever stepping out of the house

INGREDIENTS

2	broilers	cut into small pieces
1	onion	medium, finely diced
2 1" pieces	cinnamon	
1 1" piece	fresh ginger	minced
1 sprig	curry leaves	
2–3 pieces	rumpé*	
3 2" pieces	lemon grass	bruised
3 Tablespoons	tomato paste	
2 teaspoons	fenugreek**	roasted
5 cloves	garlic	minced
3	whole cloves	
3 pods	cardamom	
2 teaspoons	salt	
2 teaspoons	black pepper	
2 teaspoons	crushed chillies	(reduce to suit your taste)
1 teaspoon	turmeric powder	
2–3 Tablespoons	curry powder	roasted
2–3 cups	hot water or white wine	
2 Tablespoons	Olive oil or Canola oil	
2 Tablespoons	lemon juice & rind of one lemon	
2 Teaspoons	Balsamic vinegar	

* Available in Sri Lankan or Asian grocery stores.
** If your kids don't like biting into the fenugreek in the gravy (& mine didn't like either), add it to the roasted condiments to be powdered.

PREPARATION

- Wash & cut broilers into small pieces, drain well, & mix with salt & pepper, lemon juice and lemon rind, & set aside.
- Heat oil in a wide & deep sauce pan, at medium high.

- Add curry leaves, fenugreek, garlic, onions, rumpé, lemon grass & ginger, & sauté, stirring, until you get a nice spicy aroma.
- Add the cloves & cardamom, & stir.
- Add chicken pieces gradually, in one layer, ensuring that they get coated in the onion mixture.
- Cover, & let cook for 5 – 6 minutes.
- Uncover, & add turmeric, & coat the chicken pieces well.
- Increase heat to high, & get chicken sizzling.
- Sprinkle roasted curry powder. Make sure each piece is coated with the curry powder. Stir, mixing well. Cover, & let cook for another 5 – 6 minutes.
- Uncover, stir the sizzling chicken. Move chicken to the sides of the pan, making room in the center. When the juices start flowing into the center, add tomato paste, & let cook in chicken juices.
- Coat chicken pieces with the tomato mix. Stir well.
- Add hot water or white wine gradually, deglazing the pan & incorporating tomato paste with chicken juices & the browned gravy. Always add water into the sides of the cooking pan.
- Taste for seasoning & level of spiciness. If too spicy, add hot water gradually; if you want spicier, add more chillie powder now. Stir well. Cover, turn down the heat & let cook for a few more minutes (5 to 6). To be authentic, sprinkle dark roasted curry powder at this point. (It'll give a nice aroma & heavenly flavour.)
- As the tomato paste tends to thicken, & stick to the bottom of the pan, keep deglazing until you get the desired texture of the gravy.

A few points to remember:

o You can always adjust the seasoning to suit your palate - spicy, mild or bland gravy, thick or thin or 'tomatovy';

o Do not add water at the beginning stage of cooking. Let the chicken pieces render juice, & blend with the aromatic spices. Shhh! That's the secret to a great chicken curry!

o Be with the chicken all the time, until the heat is turned off.

o This curry can be stored in the fridge for up to a week or so. If frozen, it'll retain its flavour up to at least a month. Try your luck, & it still give you a good taste, even after.

o Don't be surprised that the chicken curry tastes better with each passing day!

SERVING SUGGESTIONS

- A full menu first
  - steamed Basmati rice;
  - parsley salad;
  - curried green beans;
  - murunga (drumsticks) white curry (Recipe in this book); &
  - pappadum.
- With roti or naan, & a chopped salad.
- With kiributh 'milkrice' (Recipe in this book)

NOTE

For better results, rub chicken pieces with the spice mixture & lemon juice, and leave in fridge to marinate overnight.

VEAL LIVER CURRY

I always choose grain-fed calf liver. Fresh, of course.

INGREDIENTS

¾ lb	calf liver	cut into bite-size pieces
3 cloves	garlic	minced
1 1" piece	cinnamon	
1 pod	cardamom	
1 sprig	curry leaves	
1 1" piece	lemongrass	fresh, bruised & sliced
1	onion	medium, finely sliced
1	green chillies	diced
1 teaspoon	sea salt or kosher salt	
3 teaspoons	black pepper	freshly ground
1 teaspoon	mustard powder	freshly ground
2 teaspoons	coriander	roasted, freshly ground
1 teaspoon	cumin	roasted, freshly ground
2 teaspoons	chillie powder	
2 teaspoons	curry powder	roasted
¼ teaspoon	turmeric	
3 Tablespoons	fat-free plain yogurt	
2 Tablespoons	Canola oil	
2 Tablespoons	coconut milk powder	
¼ cup	hot water	

PREPARATION

- Place prepared liver pieces in a ceramic dish, & add salt, pepper, coriander, cumin, turmeric, mustard powder, chillie powder & yogurt. Mix well & set aside.
- In a saucepan, @ medium high, heat oil. Add onion, garlic, curry leaves, lemongrass, cinnamon, green chillies & cardamom. Sauté, stirring.
- Add liver mixture & stir well. Cover , & cook for 2 to 3 minutes .
- Mix coconut milk powder, with the hot water until smooth. Pour into the liver mixture. Stir well. Cook for 1 to 2 minutes . Check for seasoning. Give a squirt of lemon juice if needed.
- Turn off the heat.

SERVING SUGGESTIONS

- On a bed of steamed rice.

Meat Curries

Swarna up on the Rock Fortress of Sigiriya in Sri Lanka, where the ceiling is adorned with hundreds of frescoes

An Impromptu Meal of Four Dishes

Using fridge leftovers, with salmon steaks just bought.

ชิ

ONE
SALMON STEAKS

INGREDIENTS

2 fresh salmon steaks		
½	med. white onion	diced
½	med. red onion	diced
3 cloves	garlic	minced
2 Tablespoon	Olive oil	
4	cremini mushrooms	minced
2 teaspoon	lemon rind	
2 Tablespoon	lemon juice	
salt & pepper to taste		
½ teaspoon	cayenne pepper, or ancho pepper	
1 Tablespoon	chopped parsley	
2	fresh plum tomatoes	chopped

PREPARATION

- Heat a sauté pan at medium heat.
- Add one tablespoon of Olive oil & the minced garlic.
- Add diced onions, salt & pepper.
- Stir & cook uncovered, until the mushrooms are ready (say, 2 mts.).
- Add mushrooms & stir.
- Move mushrooms to the side of the pan.
- Place the steaks in the middle of the pan, & sprinkle some Olive oil.
- Cover & let cook for about 3 minutes.
- Uncover & add the diced tomatoes & minced lemon rind.
- Turn over the steaks & cook covered for another 3 minutes.
- Turn down the heat, & if necessary, add one teaspoon of Olive oil or a dab of butter.
- Turn off the heat & leave the pan on the burner with lid on.

TWO
ROASTED POTATOES & BUTTERNUT SQUASH
In butter milk & herb dressing.

INGREDIENTS

4-6	mini red potatoes	washed (for an eye-pleasing effect, remove a thin strip of skin around the center!)
½	butternut squash	cut into big (1 x 1) cubes
1 teaspoon	Olive oil	
¼ teaspoon	each of salt & pepper	

PREPARATION

- Pre-heat oven to 400.
- Mix ingredients together.
- Bake uncovered for about 25 – 30 minutes.
- Put in a bowl.
- Pour the dressing over with a good whirl to mix the vegetables & the dressing*, & set aside at room temperature.

DRESSING

1 Tablespoon	Olive oil
1 teaspoon	Dijon mustard
1 pinch	salt
¼ teaspoon	pepper
2 teaspoons	lemon juice
4 Tablespoons	butter milk
2 teaspoons	honey
¼ cup	fresh cut herbs (parsley, minced, basil, thyme, etc.)

This evening I had the luxury of having a sous-chef in the kitchen. He mixed the dressing for me while I was busy shredding the kale for my next dish!

THREE
KALE

INGREDIENTS

1/3	bunch of kale	washed, cleaned & shredded
pinch	salt & pepper	
¼ teaspoon	sesame oil	
¼ teaspoon	Olive oil	
1 teaspoon	gourmet rice vinegar	
2 Tablespoons	hot water	
1 teaspoon	crushed chillies	

PREPARATION

- Heat a sauté pan & add the Olive oil.
- Add shredded kale immediately. Stir well.
- Add salt, pepper & crushed chillies. Continue to stir.
- Cover & let cook for 2 minutes.
- Uncover add rice vinegar & hot water.
- Cover & cook for another 3 minutes.
- Uncover, & test for doneness; let cook for another minute until water is all evaporated.
- Perfume the kale with a grate of fresh nutmeg.
- Mix well, & serve on to a platter.

NOTE

Do not cover. We eat with our eyes first; we want the colour green to stay bright!

FOUR
BASMATI, WITH WILD RICE

We really enjoyed this meal, maybe specially because it was so impromptu using leftovers!

INGREDIENTS

Leftover Basmati rice
Wild rice
Kale
Roasted pine nuts

PREPARATION

- Pop the leftover Basmati, mixed with wild rice, in the Microwave.
- Before taking it to the table, place the cooked kale on the bed of just heated rice.
- For flavour & good taste, add a Tablespoon of roasted pine nuts over the cooked kale.

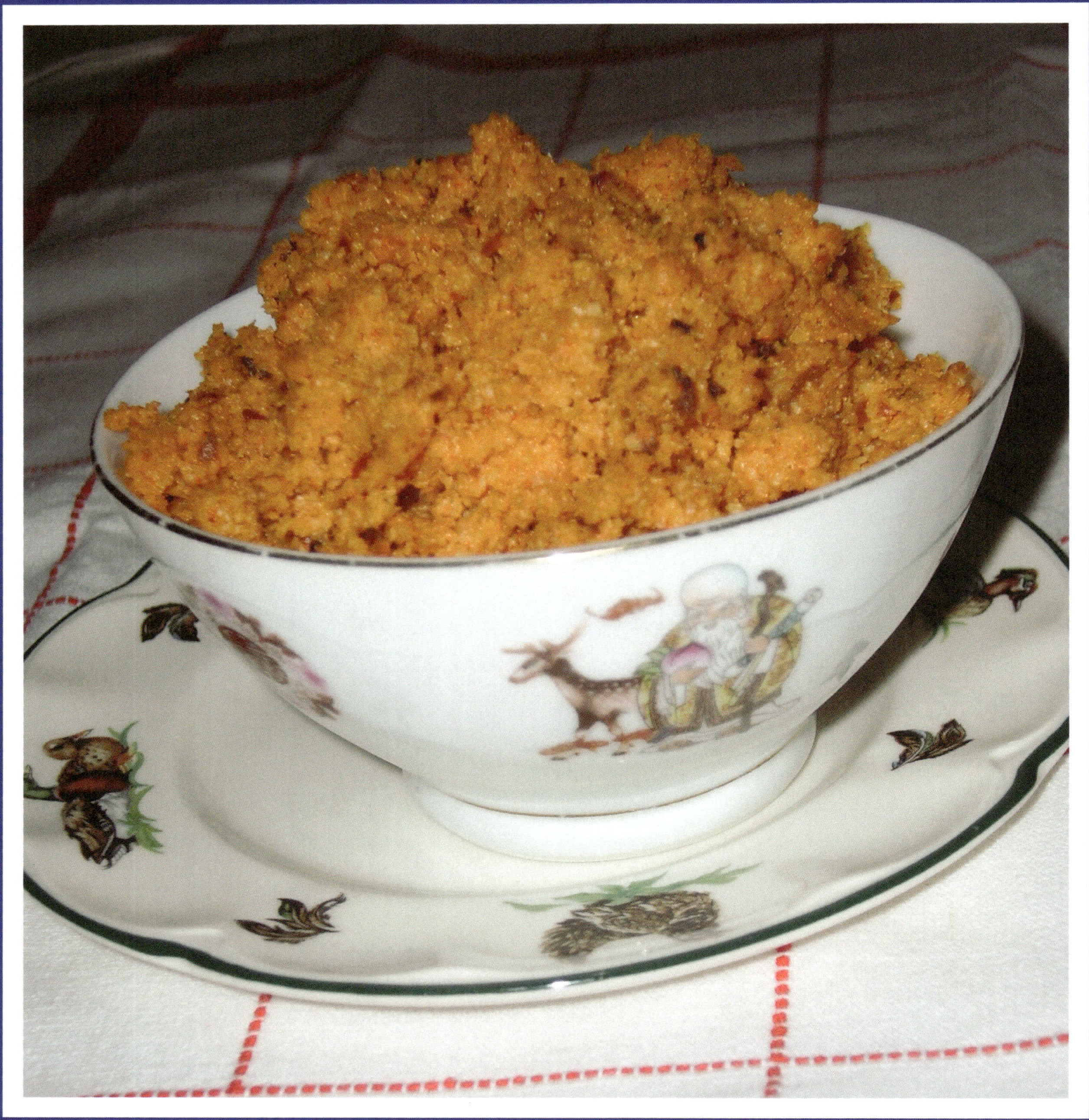

Sambols

CARROT SAMBOL
LUNUMIRIS SAMBOL
OKRA SAMBOL
POL SAMBOL
SEENI SAMBOL (REGULAR)
SEENI SAMBOL – WITH SAUTÉED JAPANESE EGGPLANTS

ඨ

CARROT SAMBOL

A refreshing, nutritious & colourful meal accompaniment.

INGREDIENTS

5	medium carrots	(preferably organic)
1	purple onion	finely diced
1	green chillie	seeded & diced
½	a lemon	juiced
¼ cup	dried cranberries	chopped (optional)
¼ cup	freshly grated coconut*	
1 Tablespoon	Maldive fish chips	
1 teaspoon	salt	
1 teaspoon	pepper	

* See Recipe for Pol Sambol for instructions.

PREPARATION

- Wash, peel & cut carrot into big chunks.
- Put in food processor, & mince coarsely. (Do not over-process. We need the crunch!)
- Put in a bowl, & add rest of the ingredients. Using your fingers, give them all a good mix. Check for taste, add salt or lemon juice, or both, to satisfy YOUR taste buds!

SERVING SUGGESTIONS

- with a rice & curry meal, specially when there's a spicy meat or fish curry in the menu.

LUNUMIRIS SAMBOL

A colourful spicy side dish! Versatile as an accompaniment.

['u' in 'lunu' (both) as in 'put'; 'i' in miris (both) as in 'English'.

Lunumiris is a versatile side dish in Sri Lanka. It provides a great contrasting (hot, meaning spicy!) accompaniment to kiributh milk rice, served on auspicious occasions. However, it goes well with any kind of boiled yam, grated coconut joining as a partner. It may also be served with cooked dried beans. But for a poor man's meal, try it with steamed rice!

INGREDIENTS

2	onions	small, white, finely diced (OR 4 big red onions)
3 Tablespoons	crushed chillies	
2 teaspoons	chillie powder	
1 teaspoon	salt	
½	a lime	juiced (add more to balance with salt flavour)
2 Tablespoons	Maldive fish	shredded

PREPARATION

- Grind all ingredients in a small electric blender, or using a mortar and pestle. You can grind it a coarse paste or a smooth paste, depending on your taste.
- Transfer to a small jar, and refrigerate for up to 2 weeks.

SERVING SUGGESTIONS

- With cooked mung beans, always with coconut, freshly grated or from your freezer (frozen freshly grated).
- With steaming rice, always with coconut, freshly grated or from your freezer (frozen freshly grated).
- With a rice meal, as a taste enhancer.

HEALTH BENEFIT

Mung beans with lunumiris is a fine healthful meal that stabilizes the sugar level in your bloodstream, in addition to other health benefits.

OKRA SAMBOL
A cholesterol buster indeed!

INGREDIENTS

½ lb	fresh okra	(OR 1 package frozen okra)
½ teaspoon	kosher salt	
¼ teaspoon	freshly ground black pepper	
1	medium purple onion	sliced
1 Tablespoon	Maldive fish	
1 pinch	crushed chillies	(OR 1 green chillie, seeded & diced)

PREPARATION

- If fresh okra, scrub & wash in cold water.
- If frozen, no need to wash or thaw.
- Put in a microwaveable dish, put in the microwave, covered, for 2 minutes at high.
- Remove lid immediately after 2 minutes ; transfer okra into a serving platter, cut each okra in half, mix with ingredients.

SERVING SUGGESTIONS

- As a side dish, with rice or noodles, couscous, or roast meat & potatoes.

Fresh Okra

Cooked Okra

Sambols

පොල් සම්බල්

POL SAMBOL

INGREDIENTS

1	coconut	fresh, scraped
1 teaspoon	black peppercorn	
2 teaspoons	crushed chillies	
2 ¼ teaspoons	sea salt	
4 teaspoons	chillie powder	(add or subtract to your taste)
2 Tablespoons	Maldive fish chips	
2	onions	medium, chopped
1	lime	juiced
1 clove	garlic	minced
½ teaspoon	ginger	fresh, grated

PREPARATION

- In the Food Processor, grind peppercorn, chillie powder, crushed chillies, onion, garlic, ginger & salt. Stop.
- With a wooden spatula, scrape the condiments to the center of the bowl.
- Add coconut, & run the Food Processor for a few seconds until the coconut is well combined with the condiments.
- Add Maldive fish & run the Processor for another few seconds.
- Transfer sambol into a bowl, sprinkle lime juice & mix thoroughly.
- Taste for seasoning. If lime flavour is not predominant, add more lime juice & to balance the flavours, add more salt.

SERVING SUGGESTIONS

- As an enhancer for a rice meal with mild flavours.
- With warm crusty bread, and a side order of sharp cheddar cheese.

NOTE

We make pol sambal, only if & when we get a fresh-tasting coconut. Below, then, are tips on

a. How to pick a good coconut,
b. How to get the kernel out,
c. How to scrape the kernel into shreds,
d. How to make your freshly grated coconut, &
e. How to preserve the hard come-by pol sambol.

a. Picking a good coconut: a multi-sensory experience!

It is not always easy to find a good coconut (in non-tropical settings), fresh enough for a pol sambol. You need your eyes, hands & ears for it! So here's a tip to pick a good one:

- Look at the 'eyes' of the coconut, to check that the coconut is not too dry, or blemished (as e.g., dark patches).

- Use your hands to feel the weight of the coconut; heavier the better.

- Use ears, to listen to the sound of the water swishing inside as you shake it. A strong sound is a good sign. That's the one to be picked!

b. Getting the kernel out

How to get the kernel out of the hard shell in two halves, without committing violence to it, is an equally challenging task! So here's how to go about it:

- At the store, pick a heavy coconut (husk peeled off), with a healthy looking hard shell (with hair).

Sambols

(**Tip:** Shake to see if you can hear the water sloshing inside.)
- Place the coconut on an open palm.
- To split it open, give it a sharp whack, with the backside of a heavy cleaver. Turn the coconut half a circle & give another whack. Turn a quarter, then another, & one more if needed. By this time, the water will begin to drip or torrent down. (My husband loves to drink it, collected into a clean container. If it tastes good, then he says the kernel is good, too.)
- Now, give the coconut a tap with the cleaver, turning it around.

If you've done it correctly, the coconut will split open, shell and kernel together, in two neat halves.

Tip: keep a bowl beneath to collect the water; it's very tasty. The taste will tell you whether the coconut is fresh or not, or even whether it is worth scraping. Or even the smell.

If, however, after the hard whacks, the hard shell opens leaving the kernel intact, turn the cleaver around, & split it in the middle (still collecting the water, if you like, for a fresh drink).

Splitting open the coconut

If upon opening you find the coconut either too dry, or smelly, a visit to the store will give you a second chance. Hopefully, this time luckier.

Now I know what you're thinking. What a bother! Much easier to get the desiccated stuff, ready on the shelf. But, believe you me, it's nowhere close to the milky flavour of the freshly grated real thing.

Sambols

c. Scraping the coconut into shreds

Nowadays, coconut scrapers, Sri Lankan style, or Indian style, are readily available in Sri Lankan or Indian stores. All you have to do is take it home, & screw it down onto your workbench.

Hold a split coconut half in one hand, and pressing it against the rotor blade, keep turning the scraper handle, turning coconut as you go. Watch to make sure you only scrape the white flesh, and not the brown layer sticking to the shell. Do the same with the other half.

Voila, you have a bowlful of milky fresh grated coconut.

Tip: Scrape it the same day as you buy it.

d. Making your freshly grated coconut go far:

Fill a small freezer bag with the pol sambol (or the freshly grated coconut), & flatten it very thin. This makes it easier to retrieve just the right amount needed for a particular use, & the remainder could be put back into the freezer. It will keep fresh for a number of months.

- Pack in small freezer bags, flattened to cover the full area of the bag. (This is to facilitate easy retrieval of just what you need for each use.) Frozen in bags, it will stay fresh for months. Take the bag out of the freezer, wedge out what you need into a bowl, & microwave for 10 sec. at 80.
- Thaw, add hot water, & put it in the food processor, to make instant coconut milk (for use in a curry).
- Thaw a handful, & add to a Mallung to get that fresh milky flavour.
- Add a handful to your roti mixture to make a tasty Sri Lankan roti.
- Make paeni-pol (see **Recipe** in this book), & stuff kiri-buth (see **Recipe**), or thin crepes, for an afternoon treat with tea.

Sambols

සීනි සම්බල්

SEENI SAMBOL (REGULAR)
A very versatile dish with practically any meal.

This again is a very versatile dish, and could be used with practically any meal, if you happen to like spicy caramalized onions. A favourite of mine growing up, I could eat a whole loaf of warm crusty bread with it in one sitting. But luckily, I burned off all those calories once I went out and played tag, running on one foot!

INGREDIENTS

8-10	cooking onions	medium, thinly sliced
2 Tablespoons	Maldive fish chips	(OR tiny dried shrimp)
4 teaspoons.	chillie powder	
4 1" pieces	cinnamon	
4 1" pieces	rumpé	
2 2" pieces	lemon grass	bruised
5 cloves	cardamom	bruised
5 Cloves	whole	
6 cloves	garlic	minced
10	curry leaves	broken into small pieces
1 teaspoon	granulated sugar	
2 teaspoons	crushed chillies	
2	ginger	thin slices minced
¼ cup	light vegetable oil (Canola)	
1 Tablespoon	tamarind pulp	diluted in ¼ cup warm water
1 teaspoon	sea salt	
½ teaspoon	black pepper	freshly ground

PREPARATION

- In a shallow sauté pan, heat oil at medium high.
- Add sliced onions and curry leaves, loosening onions with fingers.
- Stir and spread all over the pan to get onions well coated in the oil.
- Add cinnamon, rumpé, lemon grass, cloves, cardamoms, garlic, ginger and crushed chillies. Continue to stir cook.
- Add salt and pepper and the chillie powder. Stir well to combine all the condiments with onions.
- Add Maldive fish. Continue to cook stirring.
- Add the diluted tamarind pulp, mix well, cover and let cook on low heat for about 10-15 minutes.
- When the onions have reduced and cooked into a slightly thick chutney-like consistency, turn off the heat. Keep it covered for a few more minutes before serving.

SERVING SUGGESTIONS

- With kiributh (**see Recipe in this book**), warm country bread, or an exotic sandwich spread
- As an accompaniment for a meal of roti, pittu or string hoppers.

SEENI SAMBOL – WITH SAUTÉED JAPANESE EGGPLANTS
Simply delicious!

INGREDIENTS

2	eggplants (Japanese)	cut in half lengthwise, then into thin wedges, dusted with ½ teaspoon turmeric
4	cooking onions	medium, thinly sliced
1 Tablespoon.	Maldive fish chips (OR tiny dried shrimp)	
1 teaspoon	crushed chillies	
2 teaspoons	curry powder	home made roasted
1 teaspoon	salt	
1 teaspoon	pepper	
2 1" pieces	cinnamon	
1 sprig	curry leaves	
3-5 cloves	garlic	sliced thinly
1 teaspoon	tamarind paste	dissolved in ¼ cup warm water or warm coconut milk (powdered* or canned).
1 Tablespoon	lemon juice (OR 2 Tablespoons white wine vinegar)	
3 Tablespoons	Olive oil	(for sautéing)

* Left over coconut powder can be stored in the freezer for months.

PREPARATION

- Heat oil in a non-stick fry pan (to cut back on the fat) at medium heat. Add eggplants & stir well.
- Turn down heat to medium-high. Cook until golden brown.
- Transfer eggplants into a bowl.
- Add the Olive oil into the pan, & put the sliced onions.
- Start sautéing onions at high.
- Add spices, & stir well.
- Now add the tamarind mixture. Cover, & let cook at low heat.
- Taste, & adjust seasoning.

SERVING SUGGESTIONS

- With fried rice
- With rice sticks
- With crusty bread

Sambols

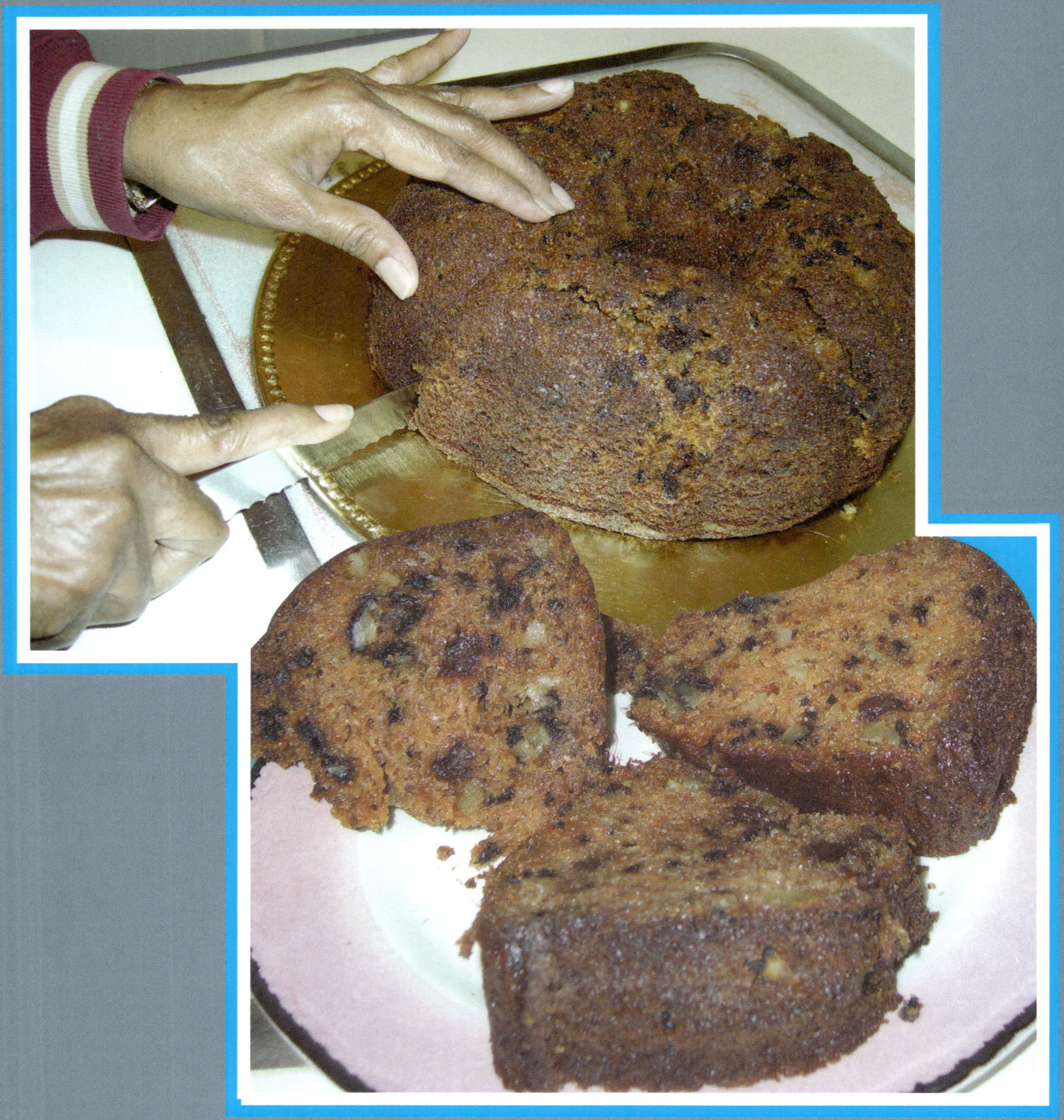

Desserts & Tea-Time Favourites

BANANA CHOCOLATE CHIP MUFFINS
PAENI-POL
SWARNA'S CARROT CAKE – A FAMILY FAVOURITE
YOGURT IN' KITUL PAENI WITH A TWIST (KIRI PAENI)

BANANA CHOCOLATE CHIP MUFFINS
A delicious and healthy snack!

INSPIRATION FOR THIS RECIPE

Shhh! don't tell him!
I came up with this recipe to satisfy my husband's sweet tooth and keep store-bought sweets away from my kitchen cabinets!

INGREDIENTS

2 cups	organic flour	
¼ cup	organic whole wheat flour	
2 teaspoons	baking powder	
1 teaspoon	baking soda	
1 teaspoon	cinnamon powder	
½ teaspoon	kosher salt	
1/3 cup	pure chocolate chips	
1/3 cup	roasted chopped walnuts	
½ cup	packed brown sugar	
1 ½ cups	ripe bananas (about 4)	mashed
1	egg	beaten
1 cup	butter milk	
¼ cup	Canola oil	
¼ cup	plain non-fat yogurt mixed with milk	

PREPARATION

- Pour wet ingredients into dry ingredients. Mix gently.
- Stir in the roasted walnuts.
- Put into lightly greased muffin cups and bake in 375^0 oven for 25 minutes.
- Take muffins out, place on a cooling wire rack for 10 minutes.
- Remove muffins from the cups and place directly on the cooling wire rack for another 10 minutes.

SERVING SUGGESTIONS

- At teatime.
- At a continental type breakfast.

පැණිපොල්

PAENI-POL
An aromatic treat!

INGREDIENTS

½	a coconut	freshly scraped
½ cup	treacle or jaggery*	
2	cardamoms	bruised (OR 1/8 teaspoon cardamom powder)
1-2 Tablespoons	coconut milk	
¼ teaspoon	fennel powder	roasted
1 pinch	salt	

* If jaggery is used, it has to be shaved into slivers and added to the coconut. (Good treacle is now readily available in Sri Lankan grocery stores.)

PREPARATION

- Mix ingredients on slow heat. Let cook.

SERVING SUGGESTIONS

- Stuffed in teatime sweet crepes.
- Stuffed in a mould of milk rice (kiributh) (see Recipe).

A very satisfying teatime snack indeed!

SWEET CREPES

INGREDIENTS

¾ cups	all purpose flour
1 teaspoon	salt
1 cup	milk (preferably whole milk)
2	eggs
2 Tablespoons	sugar
1 Tablespoon	melted butter PLUS more for cooking
½ teaspoon	vanilla extract [optional]
1 teaspoon	your favourite liqueur

PREPARATION

- Combine all ingredients in a food processor until you get a smooth batter.
- Leave the batter for half an hour.
- Heat a non-stick crepe pan to medium high.
- Pour into the centre about 2 Tablespoons of the batter and tilt the pan around until a thin crepe covering the pan surface is formed.
- Cook for 10 sec., turn, and cook for another 10 sec.
- Serve on a platter.

SWARNA'S CARROT CAKE – A FAMILY FAVOURITE
With cream cheese frosting!

CAKE:
INGREDIENTS

1¼ cups	granulated sugar
1 cup	vegetable oil
½ cup	plain no-fat yogurt
4	eggs
2 cups	all-purpose flour
2 teaspoons	baking powder
2 teaspoons	baking soda
2 teaspoons	cinnamon
1 teaspoon	kosher salt
3 cups	grated organic carrot
1 cup	chopped walnuts (toasted & broken into pieces)
1/3 cup	pure chocolate chips

PREPARATION

- Blend sugar and oil in large bowl.
- Beat in eggs, one at a time.
- Add yogurt and beat well.
- Blend the dry ingredients and stir into the sugar mixture, just until mixed.
- Stir in carrots and mix well using a spatula.
- Stir in toasted walnuts and chocolate chips.
- Pour the batter into a greased 9" x 13" baking pan and bake in a 350° oven (preheated) for 50 to 60 minutes.

FROSTING:
INGREDIENTS

1 125 g.	package cream cheese	
¼ cups	butter	melted
2 cups	icing sugar	
2 teaspoons	vanilla	
2 teaspoons	fresh lemon juice	

PREPARATION

- Using an electric mixer, whip cream cheese until fluffy.
- Beat in melted butter; then gradually add icing sugar.
- Beat in vanilla and lemon juice.
- Frost top of cake when it is completely cooled.

කිරි පැණි

YOGURT IN KITUL PAENI WITH A TWIST
A delicious & satisfying no-baking dessert!

INGREDIENTS

½ cup	Yogurt
½ cup	rice
Roasted cashew nuts*	(alternative: almonds / walnuts / pine-nuts, roasted)
Kitul paeni treacle**	(OR Canadian Maple syrup)

* Available in any food store.
** This is a Sri Lankan specialty, available in any Sri Lankan food store. Look for the MD brand to guarantee quality.

PREPARATION

This delicious dessert is ready when you're ready! No baking, no preparation.

- Take whatever amount of yogurt you're hungry for.
- Add steaming hot, or room temperature, rice, again, enough to fill your hunger.
- Add the nuts (again, as much as or as little as you want).
- Pour the kitul paeni treacle from a jar, to taste.

TIP

1. You may, of course, go for seconds, using the same amounts of each item, or varying, for a different culinary experience.
2. You may savour this as a dessert, or indeed as a hunger-filler between meals.

Many a time in Canada, I've served this with Maple syrup.

Lucky you !

If you happen to be in Sri Lanka, don't forget to try the locally made yogurt variant made of buffalo milk, called 'curd'. You'll love the taste of fresh kitul paeni poured out of a pouch of the kitul leaf itself

Desserts

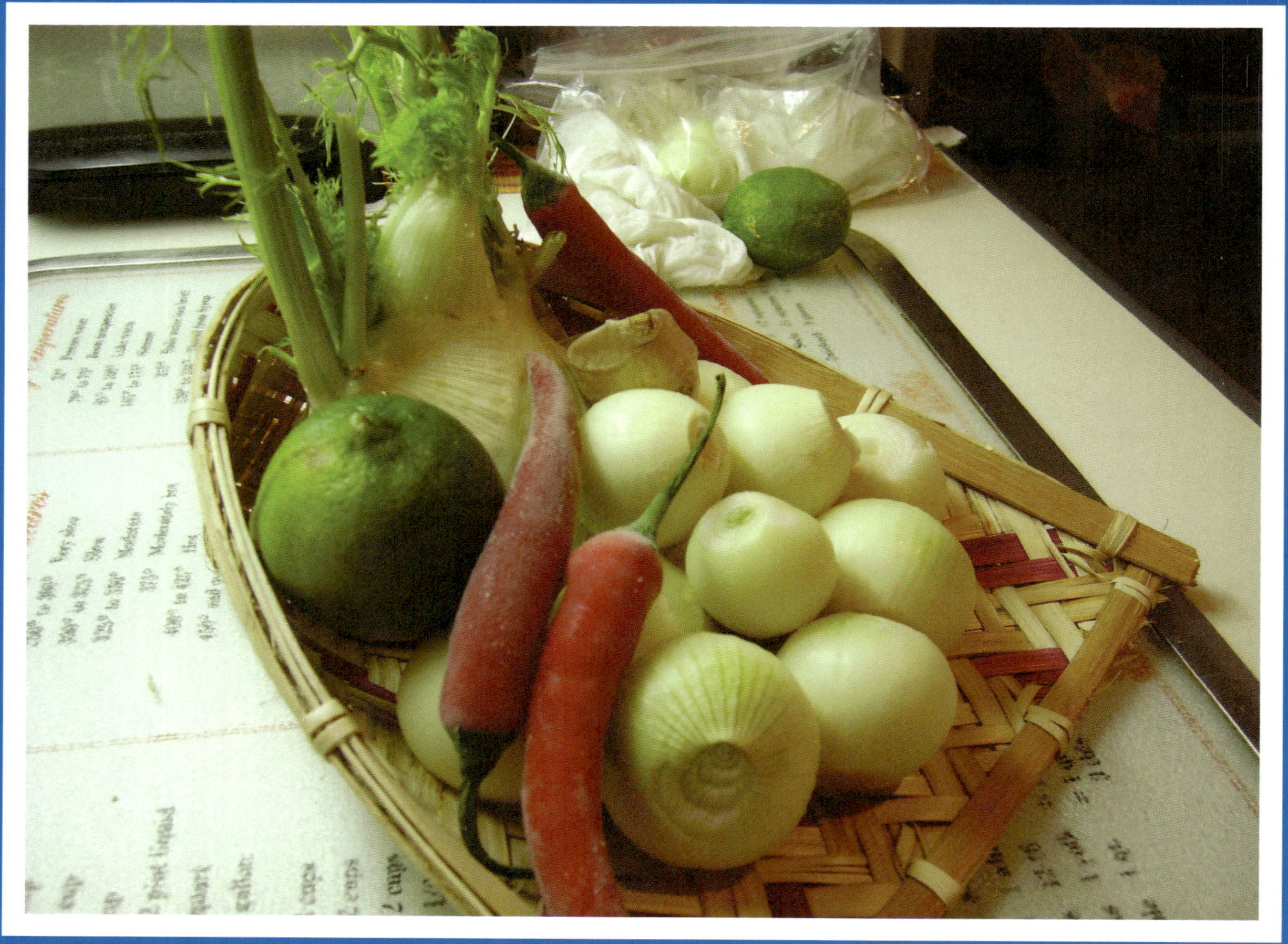

Easy Home-Made Stocks

BEEF STOCK FOR FRIED RICE
CHICKEN STOCK FOR FRIED RICE # 1
CHICKEN STOCK FOR FRIED RICE # 2

BEEF STOCK FOR FRIED RICE

INGREDIENTS

1 lb	beef & mutton bones	
8-10 cups	cold water	
4	carrots	cut into big chunks
2	celery stalks	cut into big chunks
2	onions	quartered
4 pods	cardamom	
4 cloves		
2 pieces	star anise	
1 3" piece	cinnamon stick	
1 1" thick piece	fresh ginger	
1 sprig	curry leaves (OR 2 bay leaves)	
1 teaspoon	peppercorns	
1 teaspoon	cumin seeds	
1 ½ teaspoon	sea salt	
1 Tablespoon	coriander seeds	crushed

PREPARATION

- Wash meat bones, place in a roasting pan.
- Roast at 400 until bones are dark brown.
- Turn off heat, take out bones, & place in stock pot with 8-10 cups of cold water.
- Add all ingredients, & simmer @ medium for about 2 hours.
- Drain, & use broth to make beef or mutton fried rice.

CHICKEN STOCK FOR FRIED RICE # 1
An extremely aromatic & flavourful stock!

INGREDIENTS

1	carcass of a roasted chicken	(OR 3 whole chicken legs, skinned)
4	carrots	cut into chunks
2	celery stalks	cut into chunks
½ stalk	lemon grass	
1 sprig	curry leaves	
2	green onions	cut in half
4	cloves	
2	star anise	
1 3" piece	cinnamon	
1 1" thick piece	fresh ginger	
1 teaspoon	peppercorn	
8-10 cups	cold water	

PREPARATION

- Place all ingredients in a stock pot; cover with cold water.
- Turn on heat to medium high, bring to a boil, & turn down heat; let simmer for about 1 ½ to 2 hours.
- Strain, & use stock to make fried rice.

Stocks

CHICKEN STOCK FOR FRIED RICE # 2
Will leave a distinct taste on your tongue!.

INGREDIENTS

2	medium carrots (washed)	cut in big chunks
2	celery stalks (washed)	cut in big chunks
1	medium onion	quartered
3 pods	cardamom	
3 cloves		
1 sprig	curry leaves or parsley	
5	peppercorns	whole
4	chicken drumsticks	(skinless)
1 1" chunk	peeled fresh ginger	
6 cups	cold water	
1 teaspoon	sea salt or kosher salt	

PREPARATION

- Put all ingredients in a deep pot, add water, & bring to boil.
- Turn down heat to a low simmer; let cook for 45 minutes.
- Strain the broth, & use it to cook fried rice.

This broth is so aromatic & flavourful that the rice cooked in it will leave a distinct taste on your tongue.

Stocks

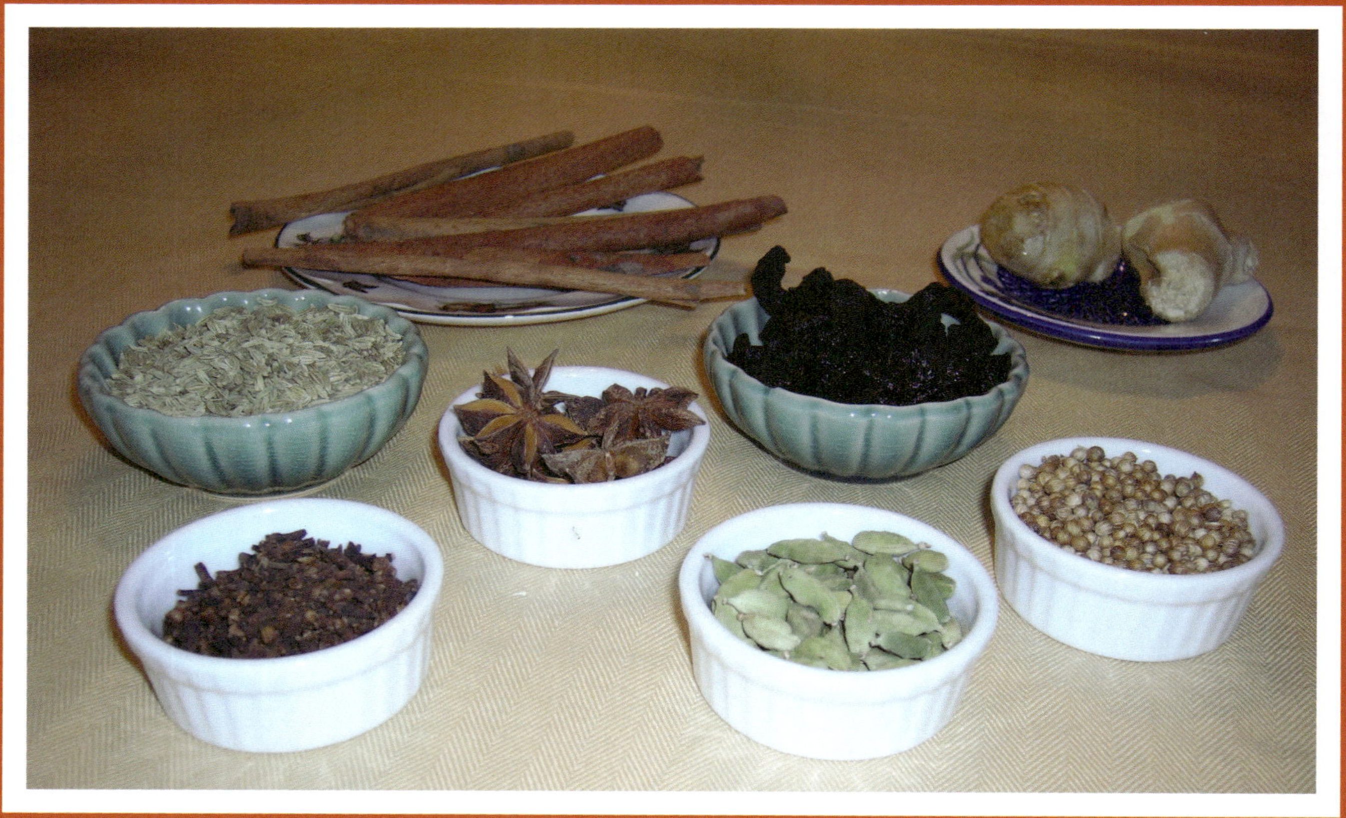

BEFORE WE GET GOING....

Spices & Combinations for Maximum Flavour

In Sri Lankan cuisine, spice condiments are blended & ground in proportions & combinations to suit each family's palate. I realized this difference in my high school days. The same fish prepared in curry form, e.g., would taste distinctly different in two different households. Our high school ran two sessions, one in the morning & another after lunch, & so, , most of us went home for a hot lunch. I was lucky to get invited often enough to my friends' homes, & this is when I began to discover the differences. Even the temparaadu, the basic sauté, had different depths of flavour. I knew which kitchens turned up the best to my liking, & as luck would have it, I also had a secret recipe to get invited! As the best student in class, who also had most comprehensive notes as well as the well-researched tutorials, more of my friends were willing to have me over.

The word curry, meaning spice condiments here, evokes different meanings, & consequently in the kitchen, allows for many a nuance for the Sri Lankan, & for that matter, even for the Indian, cook. The combinations of these spice condiments are endless. They run the whole gamut from the very basic to the painstakingly complex preparations. But it's not so difficult for an aspiring cook or a connoisseur of spicy food to find a happy middle point.

MAKING YOUR OWN CURRY POWDER

*Gives 100% better results and an authentic flavour!
Better than when you buy at the store.*

TIP:

Always buy in small quantities if you want to retain their reputed potency & the authentic flavour. Prolonged shelf life kills them both!

ALL-PURPOSE ROASTED CURRY POWDER

INGREDIENTS

3 cups	cleaned & dried coriander seeds
2 cups	cleaned & dried cumin seeds
¼ cup	fennel seeds
1 Tablespoon	fenugreek seeds
1 Tablespoon	black mustard seeds
1 teaspoon	cardamoms
1 Tablespoon	dried red chillies
2 Tablespoons	Basmati or long-grain rice
1 teaspoon	cloves
4 pieces	star anise
4 2" pieces	cinnamon
1 handful	dried curry leaves

PREPARATION

- Place a cast-iron fry pan or an old fry pan at medium low heat
- Roast all ingredients, stirring, until dark brown; let cool a bit
- Using a spice grinder, grind condiments down to a smooth powder
- Store in a sealed Mason Jar, & use as needed.

This version of roasted curry powder can be used to flavour meat, fish or vegetables, with equally good results.

Spices

BASIC SPICE CONDIMENTS
The following is a list of basic spice condiments that you must have in your pantry. Amounts shown are the recommended for one outing.

1 lb	black peppercorn	
1 cup	cardamoms	
1 lb	chillies	(dried)
¼ lb	cinnamon	(sticks)
2 oz	cloves	
1 lb	coriander	
1 lb	cumin	
½ lb	fennel	
¼ lb	fenugreek	
2-4 oz	fresh ginger	
½ lb	mustard	(black or yellow)
2 oz	nutmeg	(whole)
2 oz	star anise	(whole)
1 tub	tamarind paste	
¼ lb	turmeric	

CURRY POWDER FOR VEGETABLES

INGREDIENTS

½ cup	cleaned & dried coriander seeds
2 cups	cleaned & dried cumin seeds
1 Tablespoon	fenugreek seeds
1 Tablespoon	cleaned curry leaves (dried)
2 Tablespoons	fennel seeds
1 Tablespoon	Dried lemongrass (available in Chinese stores)
2 teaspoons	dark mustard seeds
½ teaspoon	cardamom seeds
2 3" pieces	cinnamon
4 pieces	star anise
4 cloves	

PREPARATION

- At medium-low heat, dry roast condiments in a heavy skillet until cumin seeds are golden brown. Set aside to cool.
- Using your favourite spice-grinder, reduce your condiments to a nice aromatic powder.
- Transfer into a Mason Jar, & keep covered tightly.

HINT!

√ This version of curry powder could be used with any vegetable curry.
√ For colour, add a teaspoon of turmeric powder.
√ For added kick, add a teaspoon of crushed chillies or a teaspoon of chillie powder.

EASY TO MAKE CURRY POWDER FOR STUFFINGS, DIPS OR SOUPS

This blend will add a subtle depth of flavour to your dishes.

INGREDIENTS

2 Tablespoons	cumin seeds
2 Tablespoons	fennel seeds
2 teaspoons	sesame seeds

PREPARATION

- Do a quick dry roast at medium-low. No need to wait until golden brown; just heat through to bring out the flavour.
- Grind it coarsely, using a counter top mortar & pestle.

Use as needed in dips, stuffings & salad dressings.

It is also a good rub to use on fish before grilling or pan-frying. When used on fish, add to the mixture the following:

1 Tablespoon	lemon or lime zest
1 Tablespoon	orange zest
1 Tablespoon	grated ginger
1 teaspoon	lemon or lime juice
1 teaspoon	Olive or Canola oil.

Enjoy!

GARAM MASALA

INGREDIENTS

½ cup	coriander seeds	cleaned & dried
¼ cup	cumin seeds	cleaned & dried
1 Tablespoon	fennel seeds	
1 sprig	dry curry leaves	(optional) (OR I dry bay leaf)
1 teaspoon	pepper corns	
1 teaspoon	cardamom pods	
1 teaspoon	cloves	
1 Tablespoon	broken cinnamon sticks	

PREPARATION

- In a small skillet over medium low heat, toast all ingredients until fragrant and lightly coloured.
- Grind to a fine powder.
- Store in an air tight container up to 1 month.

Spices

SPICE MIXTURE FOR OVEN FRIED NEW YORK FRIES

INGREDIENTS

½ teaspoon	cayenne pepper
1 teaspoon	freshly ground cumin powder
1 teaspoon	sweet paprika powder
1 teaspoon	chillie powder
1 teaspoon	black pepper
1 teaspoon	garlic powder
1 teaspoon	kosher salt

PREPARATION

- In a small mixing bowl mix the above ingredients & rub over the potato strips.
- Then sprinkle about 3 Tablespoon of Olive oil & bake in a baking sheet in oven pre-heated at 400.

This spice mixture is enough for 4 medium Yukon gold potatoes.

Spices

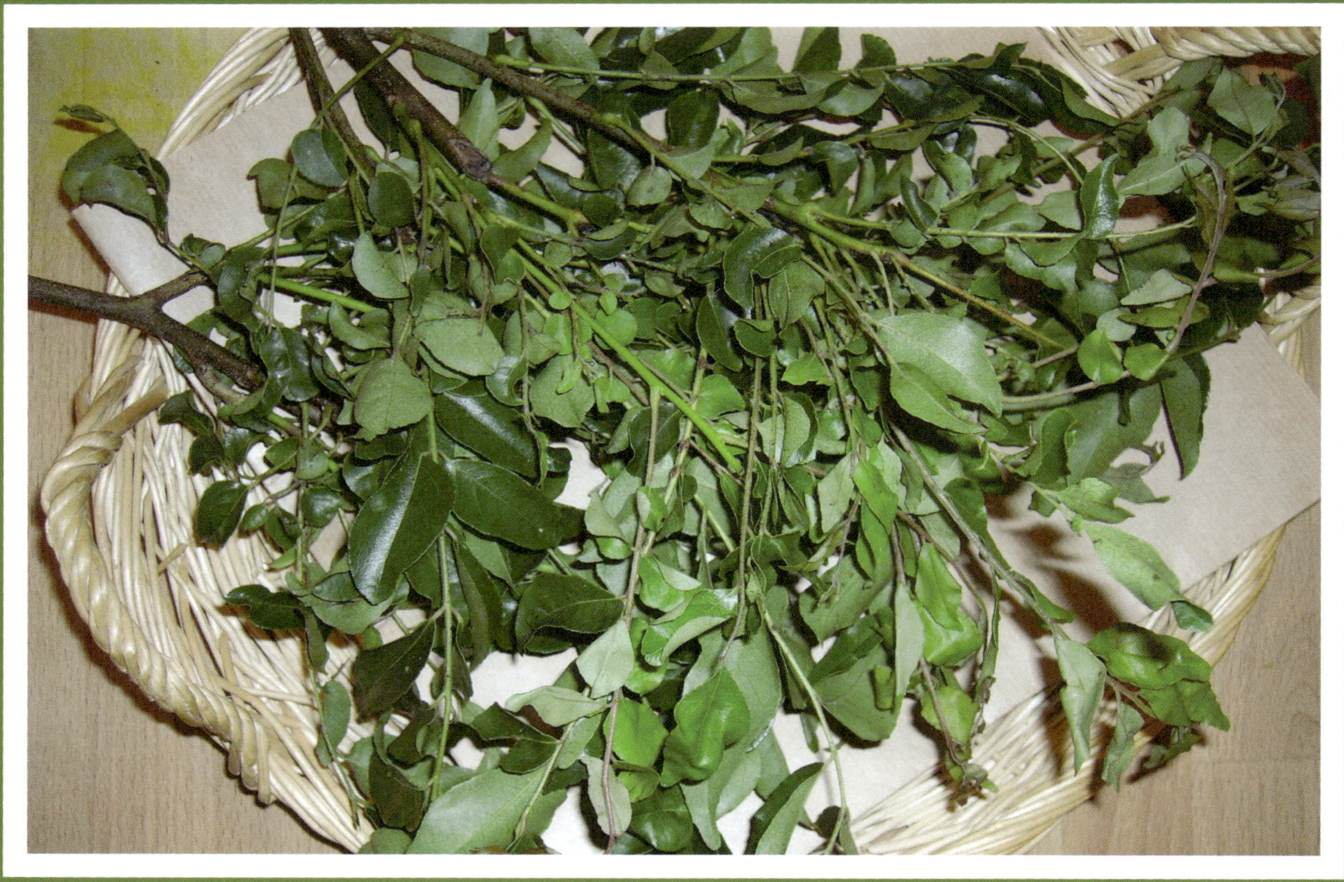

Glossary

CONDIMENTS USED IN THIS BOOK

CARDOMOM (ENSAL)

Cardamom has a pungent flavour and is used in curry powders and desserts as well as in spicy Indian tea (chai). Even though the tiny cardamom seeds are embedded inside the pod, the entire cardamom is used in making aromatic spice powders. If the entire pod is used in certain preparations like yellow rice or meat dishes, the pods are removed before serving, or eating.

CHICKPEA FLOUR

Also known as besan flour, chickpea flour is made from a variety of chickpeas and is used in batters for deep frying, as e.g., in frying cauliflower, and is mixed with ground lentils in making **lentil fritters**. (see Recipe in this book).

CHILLIE

Chillie is a basic essential in Sri Lankan cuisine. Fresh green and red chillies are used in curries, along with dried red chillie flakes and ground chillie.

CINNAMON

The cinnamon plant is native to Sri Lanka. The bark of the plant is dried and used in powder form and in small bundles cinnamon sticks. Both versions, are aromatic and flavourful. Powdered cinnamon is used mainly in desserts. Sticks are used in making roasted spice blends and are used directly in meat, fish and vegetable curries. Cinnamon sticks have long shelf life.

HEALTH TIP

Cinnamon has medicinal value as well. It's supposed to stabilize the sugar level in your blood.

CLOVES

Cloves, dried unopened flower buds, add a sweet and spicy flavour to curry powders. They are used sparingly and only in meat dishes. A few whole cloves added to yellow rice give it an added nuance of flavour.

HEALTH TIP

Growing up in Sri Lanka. we used to keep biting into a clove if our stomachs gave any sign of indigestion. It works for me even today.

COCONUT MILK

Using freshly grated coconut

First extract milk (miti-kiri)
- Transfer the scraped coconut into a pyrex jar.
- Add warm water, and mix.
- Pour the mixture into the food processor, and give it a whirl.
- Pour into a bowl using a fine strainer.

2nd and 3^{rd,} extracts (diya-kiri 'more diluted milk')
- Mix the used coconut with another cup of warm water
- Pour the mixture into the food processor, and give it another whirl.

Pour into a bowl using a fine strainer

CORIANDER

Coriander leaves are available in any of the regular food chains as folks from many cultures use it to blend with other herbs to add to chutneys or to finish cooked veggies or meats. Coriander leaves have a distinct flavour and aroma different from that of the seed. Roasted and ground coriander seeds are a key ingredient in a Sri Lankan spice mix. Even though powdered coriander is available in stores, for maximum flavour, you're better off to roast coriander seeds yourself in small amounts or grind them as you need.

CUMIN

Greenish brown cumin seeds have a smoky flavour with a dried peppermint tinge. Just like coriander, cumin is another essential for making a Sri Lankan spice blend. .

Glossary

CURRY LEAVES

This is a another basic flavour enhancer in Sinhalese curries. Curry leaves grow on a tree native to Sri Lanka, and it belongs to the same family as oranges and lemons. These aromatic leaves can be used fresh or dried. Curry leaves, together with minced garlic and diced onions form the first flavour base of a curry. When you happen to find fresh curry leaves - (bunches of fresh curry leaves in cellophane bags are available in any Indian or Sri Lankan grocery shop), you might want to buy a whole bunch or two, because they can be frozen with excellent results.

Tips on freezing curry leaves

- Fill the kitchen sink with cold water, & empty the bags into it. Rinse thoroughly, drain, & dry between tea towels.
- Cut the sprigs into pieces, using the kitchen scissors, & re-pack in empty margarine tubs.
- Keep in your fridge freezer; they'll last for months & months.
- When you need, open a tub, take a few pieces, & add directly into a sauté pan or the curry. Make sure that you put back the tub immediately. Keeping it out will result in curry leaves getting discoloured.

DRIED SHRIMP

Dried tiny shrimps have a strong flavour and are used mainly in Sambols and Mallungs (see Recipes under each heading). They are available at Asian grocery stores.

FENNEL SEED

Fennel seeds are similar in appearance to cumin seeds but have a sweet aniseed flavour. It is used primarily in roasted spice blends and in Sri Lankan desserts.

FENUGREEK

A member of the pea family, fenugreek's yellowish brown seeds are used dried in vegetable and seafood dishes. When used as a thickening agent for curries with gravy, fenugreedk seeds are soaked in water overnight and then used in the curry.

HEALTH TIP

Fenugreek seeds are known to have medicinal value to bring down high blood pressure, when taken as a tea mixed with a few slices of fresh garlic.

FRESH GINGER

If you see a really fresh ginger at a supermarket, grab a good clump, & save it in your fridge freezer.

But how?
- Wash, & cut into smaller pieces, & peel off the skin.
- Put in small freezer bags, & store. It'll last for months.
- When you need it, all you have to do is take out a piece & grate it.
- For a digestion-friendly ginger tea, slice it & put in boiling water.

GARAM MASALA

A spice mixture that is used as a flavour-enhancer in soups, dips and gravies. See Recipe.

GARLIC

ගොරක

GORAKA (GAMBODGE)

'Gambodge' is the botanical name for what the Sinhala people in Sri Lanka call 'Goraka'. It is used in cooking fish and pork curries in particular, as a souring agent similar to tamarind, and a flavour-enhancer. It has a taste similar to that of a tangerine – i.e., sweet and sour. Bright orange when ripe, goraka segments get dried and shriveled into leathery pieces in the hot tropical sun. It is this that's used in cooking, so they can be removed before eating.

How to use it:

- Wash in warm water thoroughly to get them grit-free.
- When they are soaked and soft, turn it into a paste, using an electric grinder, or the mortar and the pestle if you prefer.

The paste will last in your fridge for a number of days.

KAFFIR-LIME LEAVES

A flavour-enhancer in fish and seafood curries, these are available in East Asian grocery stores. Fresh leaves are available in small packets, and dry leaves in small plastic bags.

How to freeze them:
- Empty the bags into a sink full of cold water. Wash well. Dry between tea towels.
- Re-pack in freezer bags, & store in fridge freezer. They, too, last for ever!

The Kaffir-lime leaves add to a curry an amazingly distinct taste! Try it in a shrimp curry and check for yourself. You'll be hooked.

Glossary

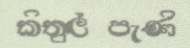

KITUL PAENI

Native to Sri Lanka, this is a syrup tapped off the kitul palm tree. Though similar to the Canadian Maple syrup, kitul paeni leaves a much more complex flavour in your tongue.

LEMON GRASS

Buy your lemon grass at any East Asian store. You'll pay only half the price, & product could be fresher.
- Wash & dry well at home. Cut into 4 inch pieces.
- Put in small freezer bags, & store. It'll last for months.
- When you need it, take out only one piece, slice it thinly or grate directly into the curry, paste, soup or the dressing.

LONG BEANS (MAE-KARAL)

The long dark green beans are popularly curried in Sri Lanka, just like green beans. Fresh long beans are readily available in Asian grocery stories.

MALDIVE FISH

Maldive fish is the dried Boneto fish, caught in the South China sea and processed on the Maldive Islands, which neighbours Sri Lanka. Maldive fish chips are used to flavour vegetable curries and heavily used to flavour sambols, such as lunumiris, seeni sambol and caramelized onions (see Recipes). They add a tongue-pleasing flavour to Mallungs as well (see Recipes).

MUSTARD SEEDS

Brown or black mustard seeds can be bought in any supermarket and is used in curries whole or ground.
- If used whole, sauté in oil with curry leaves and onions until they 'pop' to release their flavour.

PAPPADUM

Dried and packaged pappadums are available in South Asian grocery stores and in some mainstream food chains. Made of a mixture of lentils, rice, flour and salt, they, circular shaped, come in many different sizes and flavours.

- They can be fried in a shallow sauté pan with a little bit of oil at medium high heat. Pappadums take no time to crisp up. So remember to work fast when frying them. Once taken out of the pan, place them in a tray of paper towels.

- They can be kept crisp for days when sealed in a zip-lock bag.

RED RICE

Unpolished or unrefined rice which contains more fibre than polished rice. Red rice can be cooked mixed with Basmati rice with very successful results. The combination will not only turn out to be of high nutritional value, but also rich in flavour.

Glossary

RUMPÉ (PANDANUS)

The stiff bright green pandanus leaf is used for its flavour in curries and rice dishes. There is no substitute for the usual nutty, grassy flavour of the leaf which is cut into pieces and added to a dish but removed prior to eating, or saved as a garnish but not eaten.

- There is no particular preparation, except the size of the piece, identified in each Recipe.

TAMARIND

Tamarind is native to many countries, including Sri Lanka. Tamarind pods grow on branches of a huge tree, and when the pods ripen, they fall off the stem and drop under the tree. As kids, we used to pick up these pods, store them in our lunch boxes and eat with sea salt! The sweet and sour taste of a tamarind pod is an amazing flavour enhancer and a natural tenderizer in meat and fish dishes. Caramalized onions, flavoured with diluted tamarind paste, is a great side dish for roasted meats as well as sweet milk rice (Kiributh) (see Recipe in this book).

කහ

TURMERIC POWDER (KAHA)

This bright yellow rhizome, which looks like a small version of ginger, is used in Sri Lankan cuisine for its colour and medicinal properties. It is also used as a substitute for the more expensive saffron, in cooking yellow rice and other curries.

Shhh!

Water, coloured with turmeric, is sprinkled at Sri Lankan houses to get rid of germs.

AVAILABILITY

STORES WHERE SOME OF THE EXOTIC GROCERY ITEMS IN THE MENUS ARE AVAILABLE:

Asian	Black rice
	Bittergourd
	Dried shrimp in various sizes
	Eggplant
	Fresh Turmeric
	Kaffir Lime Leaves
	Lemon grass (both fresh and dried)
	Long beans
	Okra
	Red Rice
	Rumpé
Indian	All spices
	Bittergourd
	Curry leaves
	Ghee
	Murunga
	Pappadum
	Methi
Sri Lankan	Bittergourd (karivila)
	Coconut milk (powdered)
	Curry leaves
	Gambodge (Goraka)
	Jaggery
	Lemon grass (fresh only)
	Maldive fish
	Murunga
	Pappadum
	Raw red rice
	Rumpé
	Treacle

Glossary

Printed in the United States
131207LV00004B